Developing Quantitative Literacy Skills in History and the Social Sciences

Developing Quantitative Literacy Skills in History and the Social Sciences

A Web-Based Common Core Standards Approach

Kathleen Craver

ROWMAN & LITTLEFIELD
Lanham • Boulder • New York • London

Published by Rowman & Littlefield
A wholly owned subsidiary of The Rowman & Littlefield Publishing Group, Inc.
4501 Forbes Boulevard, Suite 200, Lanham, Maryland 20706
www.rowman.com

16 Carlisle Street, London W1D 3BT, United Kingdom

British Library Cataloguing in Publication Information Available

Library of Congress Cataloging-in-Publication Data

Craver, Kathleen W.
Developing quantitative literacy skills in history and the social sciences : a web-based common core
standards approach / Kathleen Craver.
p. cm.
Includes bibliographical references and index.
ISBN 978-1-4758-1050-9 (cloth : alk. paper) -- ISBN 978-1-4758-1051-6 (pbk. : alk. paper) -- ISBN
978-1-4758-1052-3 (electronic)
1. Social sciences--Statistical methods--Study and teaching. 2. Social sciences--Methodology--Study
and teaching. 3. History--Statistical methods--Study and teaching. 4. History--Methodology--Study
and teaching. 5. Web-based instruction.
HA35.C66 2014
300.71'073--dc23
                                                                                        2014018105

Printed in the United States of America

To Charlie whose faith and confidence has always sustained me.

Contents

Acknowledgments

I wish to thank Professor David Barnes for his kind assistance with the charts and figures in this book. I would also like to thank my wonderful colleague James Lucas for his unbelievable patience, sense of humor, and tact as he helped me wrestle various charts into acceptable word processing formats. The persistent encouragement of my husband, Charlie, has been invaluable. I gratefully acknowledge the advice, enthusiasm, and support that my editors, Tom Korerner and Carlie Wall, gave me throughout this exciting project. I would finally like to express my appreciation to Production Editor Chris Basso and Copy Editor Katy Whipple for their highly professional assistance.

Preface

Math anxiety is a real fear among most history and social science educators. The aversion to it is usually one of the main reasons why history and social science educators elect to major in the humanities rather than the physical sciences in college. If you are concerned about how to satisfy the National Common Core Standards for history and social sciences, which requires students to be able to integrate quantitative or technical analysis in the form of charts, research data, and graphs, and to address historical questions or solve problems with the data, then rest assured that this book has been written for you. The quantitative information and accompanying questions are designed to require no mathematical skills beyond eighth grade.

Being charged with the responsibility that our students become quantitatively literate has long been the sole domain of those teaching mathematics. In the data-drenched world of the current century, however, it has now become the responsibility of not only history and social science educators but also STEM (science, technology, engineering, and mathematics) coordinators and curriculum development specialists to integrate quantitative literacy skills into all aspects of the school curriculum, including the humanities.

National and international studies continue to show that the United States has fallen behind other developed countries on assessments involving critical thinking with numbers, data, and other quantitative information. The introduction of Common Core Standards and their adoption by a majority of states is the final educational green light to introduce numeracy skills to ensure that our students possess the ability to pose quantitative questions evident in historical and social sciences sources, read and interpret representations of various types of quantitative information, and produce accurate numerical and visual displays of data.

The purpose of this book is to provide history and social sciences educators with sound pedagogical techniques and critical thinking questions and activities to introduce their students to a fascinating selection of multicultural and multi-century valid and reliable Internet sites. The sites contain a wealth of quantitative information in the form of lists, tables, charts, and graphs. Because so many primary and secondary sources are no longer protected by copyright, academic libraries, archives, and other educational institutions are continuing to digitize them and post them on the Web.

Even more important is the search software that accompanies these sites. Students who years ago had to be satisfied with citing one table or graph from a textbook now have quantitative data at various historical and social sciences megasites, rivalling those at large universities, at their electronic fingertips. Many of these quantitative social sciences sites even contain built-in graphing capabilities.

The implications for incorporating historical and social sciences quantitative information by using critical thinking skills are widespread. It means that history and social science educators are no longer bound to the classroom-textbook-lecture method. They can infuse their courses with exciting, stimulating historical and quantitative sources that can make their respective subjects come alive.

As an author of five books dealing with library science and historical primary sources, and working as a head librarian in a prominent, college-bound independent school, I have had the opportunity to observe how students undertake history and social science assignments that involve any form of quantitative information. Even when students discover numerical historical or social sciences sources that will clearly provide them with an excellent thesis for a major term paper, I hear the constant refrain, "I can't use this information because there's math in it." I have even watched their outstanding teachers shy away from recommending a source that contains historical or social science evidence in the form of lists or tables because they did not feel comfortable guiding a student through the research and thesis development process with numbers rather than words.

Since I work with the same educators and students throughout extended periods in the library, assisting them in finding interesting and challenging historical and social sciences sources either in print or on the Internet, it occurred to me to use a Web-based approach to introduce teachers, and through them their students, to the cornucopia of quantitative sources that exist within valid and reliable Internet sites.

Even though I wrote this book primarily for history and social science teachers, I also had their students in mind. While the first two chapters of the book feature basic instructions for how to use, interpret, display, and visualize quantitative sources, the third part, comprising chapters 3, 4, and 5, contains a multitude of quantitative web sites, each supplying a set of specific, site-related critical thinking questions. From past experience, each topic was carefully selected to be of interest to secondary school students, including sites about piracy, witchcraft, biological warfare, and natural disasters.

I wrote the book so that history and social science educators can use the sites as lesson plans and activities when teaching a certain area, assign them to a class to meet Common Core quantitative literacy requirements, or recommend a site to an individual student who may be mathematically inclined. Some teachers may also wish to make the book available as an additional potential term paper resource book.

It is my fervent wish that history and social science educators can use this book to easily embrace the National Common Core Standards requirement for quantitative literacy in the humanities. I want them to feel comfortable guiding their students to use numbers as evidence in history and the social sciences, and to never experience a moment's math anxiety with them.

Introduction

THE NEED FOR INSTRUCTIONAL CHANGE

The instructional role of history and social science educators is being influenced not only by advances in technology but also by economic, educational, and employment changes. When Elliot Schrage, current vice-president of communications for Facebook and past communications director of Google, was asked at an in-house presentation to education and publishing executives what discipline students should be urged to study, his unhesitating reply was "statistics, because the ability to understand data would be the most powerful skill in the twenty-first century" (Freeland, 2012, 47).

Schrage's 2009 recommendation appears to be the correct one as more and more corporations and government organizations depend upon a multitude of online databases and datasets to influence and direct their decisions. With expanded access and increased storage and retrieval capabilities, databases have grown to enormous sizes ranging from terabyte, or one thousand gigabytes, to petabytes, or one thousand terabytes. Wal-Mart's database, for example, contains more than 570 terabytes (Ayres, 2007, 10–11). The world is awash in Internet data that is available twenty-four/seven from almost any location in the world.

Viewing the globe as containing unfathomable amounts of historical or social sciences data presents students with an outlook on the humanities that they may never have considered. As our society becomes more numerate because of powerful computers crunching massive quantities of analog and digital data, students will need quantitative literacy skills to analyze documents and historical evidence in different ways (Mayer-Schonberger and Cukier, 2013, 97). Introducing them to historical and contemporary charts, graphs, and other visual information formats from a variety of sources dating back even to the 1600s and having them create their own information displays based on quantitative data will help prepare them for a world that will demand higher numeracy skills than in previous decades.

For students taking history and social science courses, the Web is a virtual treasure trove to research and mine for assignments and term papers. Yet studies show that students, despite the recommendations from 2012 Common Core State Standards Initiatives, seem reluctant to employ quantitative data either centrally or peripherally in humanities-related assignments. The standards stress that students in grades nine to twelve should be able to "integrate quantitative or technical analysis (e.g., charts, research data) with qualitative analysis and analyze quantitative information to address a question or solve a problem" (Common Core State Standards Initiative, 2012).

Many students are departing high school with a level of quantitative literacy that is far below the minimum expectations not only for continuing education but also for any type of gainful employment. Seeing patterns in data, interpreting statistics, and presenting it in various quantitative formats have become de rigueur for most businesses but not formally required by high schools and many times higher education institutions. These abilities are considered essential components of the definition of quantitative literacy (Steen, 2000, 8–9).

RESPONDING TO THE WORKPLACE

It is imperative that history and social science educators require students to use readily available quantitative data to meet their future educational and employment needs. Quantitative literacy is one of the necessary elements to work in one of the fastest growing and remunerative occupations in a workplace characterized by constant change. The U.S. Department of Labor notes that the information technology industry is one of the economy's booming sources of workplace growth. The projected 2004-2014 technology employment increase of 453,000 new jobs will result in a total of 1.6 million jobs. The hiring of computer and information systems managers is estimated to grow between 18 to 26 percent for all occupations through the year 2014 (High Growth Industry Profile Information Technology, 2010).

There are several downsides, however, to this optimistic estimate. The first negative aspect concerns the ability of corporations to outsource some of these jobs to countries where the wages are significantly lower. These jobs are within a globally competitive category, thus placing them at more risk. The second converse is a form of global competition caused by the educational inadequacy of our current population.

Because the need for technology workers is so great, some companies such as Google, Microsoft, and Facebook claim to be experiencing trouble hiring qualified workers because of visa limits. The U.S. Congress is considering creating an immigration plan that would allow and grant permanent legal status to an unlimited number of students who earn graduate degrees from U.S. universities in science, technology, engineering, or math (Wallsten, 2003, A4-5). While educated, skilled workers are welcome in any country, in a globally competitive job market, it seems tragic that members of the indigenous population are not qualified or educated sufficiently to work in these positions.

Employers are also indicating that the level of higher order thinking skills is to too low to satisfy the demands of the new information economy. Members of the U.S. 21st Century Workforce Commission have testified that they are seriously troubled that high school graduates cannot perform the mathematical computations required for additional study and training in science, technology, engineering, and mathematical occupations. Acquiring logical thinking and problem-solving skills is a prerequisite for entrance into post–high school information technology programs (U.S. 21st Century Workforce Commission, 2000, 69).

As more companies and businesses produce non-tangible products, they desire employees who can see patterns in information, manipulate data, and represent the information graphically. Occupations representing information age jobs include computer engineers, architects, systems analysts, database administrators, computer support specialists, accountants, graphic artists, Web designers, electrical engineers, technology support, and network managers.

MAKING THE CONNECTION

Most employment specialists note that a much larger percentage of workers will need these same quantitative skills just to survive as more occupations become increasingly technologically advanced. The level of education workers attain is strongly related to their income level. In the next five to ten years, this equation will have a distressing impact upon those who are unable or unwilling to heed it. Already about 75 percent of information technology positions require quantitative literacy skills at least at the bachelor's degree level. It is only the remaining 25 percent of information technology occupations that are projected to require an associate's degree.

The correlation between education and income level is a positive one. Employment statistics show that the absence of a college degree will probably doom most U.S. workers from achieving a decent standard of living. The education versus income gap has been accelerating in recent decades. In 1975, the average college graduate earned 57 percent more than the typical high school graduate. In 1997, the average college graduate earned $40,478, which represented 77 percent more than the typical high school graduate's earnings of $22,895 (U.S. 21st Century Workforce Commission, 2000, 27).

By 2018, 63 percent of jobs are projected to require postsecondary education beyond high school (Carnevale, Smith, and Strohl, 2010, 5). Contrast this percentage to that of 1959 when only 20 percent of jobs held by workers required some postsecondary education, and one readily comprehends what a lack of education and critical thinking skills portends for high school graduates (U.S. 21st Century Workforce Commission, 2000, 27). Although many employers could have filled positions vacated by high school graduates with other high school graduates, a significant percentage chose instead to hire college graduates.

Economists believe that they were responding to increased competition and to the way work was being performed. Some companies, for example, outsourced high school–level work and hired college graduates for financing and marketing tasks. Other companies introduced advanced technologies such as robotics that require better-educated workers to operate machines. The estimated cost to finding highly skilled employees and raising new workers' skill levels worldwide is estimated at more than $200 billion per year (Trilling and Fadel, 2012, 7).

OBTAINING THE SKILLS

What are the skills that high school graduates need to increase their wages? In 1991, Robert Reich, former Secretary of Labor, published a seminal, prophetic book titled *The Work of Nations*. In it, he advocated for centering education around a "lifetime of symbolic-analytic work." A symbolic-analyst combines four critical thinking skills: abstraction, system thinking, experimentation, and collaboration (Reich, 1991, 227).

To think abstractly means to be able to discern patterns or meanings in data so that it can be equated, formulated, analyzed, or categorized. This abstract process of construing data into usable patterns is characteristic of all of the projected twenty-first century fastest-growing occupations. All of these growth occupations have been associated with decent standards of living.

System thinking, a more advanced stage of abstraction, requires that individuals be able to recognize patterns and meaning and how they relate to a complex process or cycle. Problems are identified and then linked to other problems. The use of DDT and its deleterious concatenated connection to an entire ecosystem of animals and plants is illustrative of system thinking.

Experimentation, rarely used as a teaching method in most disciplines with the exception of science, is needed to establish cause and effect, similarities and differences, and possibilities and outcomes. This method can easily be adapted and applied to historical research and social sciences problems and issues. It is a form of thinking that provides opportunities for students to use tools to structure their own learning situations.

Last is the ability to collaborate, work in teams, and to share information and solutions. The means to accomplish this can be provided through oral reports, designs, developing web sites, creating online time lines, producing sophisticated graphs and charts, hosting discussions, and fostering debates. The emphasis on this form of learning—using critical thinking skills instead of mere acquisition of unrelated facts—is to stimulate the type of thinking that will be needed to achieve success in a technologically advanced global marketplace (Craver, 1994, 67–68).

Although critical thinking skills will be essential to meet the educational, employment, and technological demands of the twenty-first century, they do not come naturally to the untrained mind. In his book, *Critical Thinking: What Every Person Needs to Survive in a Rapidly Changing World*, Richard Paul states that the mind is "instinctively designed for habit, associating 'peace of mind' with routine" (Paul, 1993, v). According to Paul, the mind is naturally inclined to simplify the complex and to make things recognizable in familiar, well-ordered patterns.

His thoughts on this subject are reinforced in several national educational assessments. They show that in every subject, American students can perform basic tasks successfully, but they do not score well on parts that measure thinking and reasoning skills. In mathematics, American students can compute, but not reason. As quantitative methods have become an integral part of employment and even basic life, they have also begun to assume a more dominant role in education.

Mathematics is no longer the sole province of scientists and engineers; some aspect of quantitative literacy is mandated of almost anyone entering the information technology workforce or seeking promotion in a profession or occupation. Online newspapers, e-zines, and web sites are replete with charts, graphs, and references to percentages and numbers that require a quantitative literate population to have the knowledge to make informed decisions as voters and consumers (Steen, 2000, 9).

RETHINKING THE TEXTBOOK APPROACH

One factor that may contribute to these poor test results is the textbooks that students are using to obtain their information. While the materials in them are factually correct, textbooks are designed to cover large amounts of material superficially. To achieve this goal and reach a broad market in different states, authors must avoid analysis and resist the desire to pose questions or activities that would require critical thinking skills that incorporate quantitative methods. History texts need to include as much material about as many historical periods as possible.

For years, history educators had to be content with the textbook approach because their school libraries lacked the funds and storage space to stock large amounts of primary and even secondary source materials. With the advent of the Internet, however, this is no longer the case. Now history and social science educators have a wealth of primary historical and social sciences sources available online and can easily utilize a Web-based approach to their instruction.

REQUIRED HARDWARE, SOFTWARE, AND EXPERTISE

It is preferable to have a classroom set of computers that are loaded with Microsoft Excel and word processing software. Excel will allow students to display some of the quantitative data sites that they research in chart or graph formats. Word processing software is helpful for creating tables for other forms of data. Some of the sites are equipped with software that allows students to create and display data in graph or chart form within the site and download it to their own computers.

For performing calculations, students can be referred to Wolfram Alpha (www.wolframalpha.com/). It accepts natural querying language for posing mathematical questions such as, "What is 10 percent of 2,500?" Chapter 3 contains references to a number of free charting and graphing sites that students can use as well.

Most humanities teachers may wince at the thought of using quantitative data, but this book is meant to disabuse them of this idea. The majority of quantitative literacy researchers have declared that the type of data students need to think critically requires only an eighth-grade education. While the author is aware of history researchers at universities who work with large datasets and use software packages to crunch it such as Software Program for the Social Sciences, the deliberate intention of this book is to have students successfully learn to integrate quantitative data into non-mathematical courses so that they become better critical thinkers and comfortable working with numbers in addition to textual sources.

There are repositories of historical and social sciences sources that contain evidence in the form of quantitative data that students should be made aware. While some of the included sites are particularly robust with data and are amenable to more sophisticated statistical analysis, a deliberate choice was made to avoid using these methods. The goal of this book is create a comfort and confidence level for history and social science teachers so that they will continue to expose their students to quantitative sources and develop their critical thinking skills.

BOOK ARRANGEMENT AND RECOMMENDED USE

The book is arranged in five chapters. Chapter 1 presents an overview of quantitative literacy. It discusses the definitional aspects that have occurred over the years, provides a brief summary of quantitative literacy research findings, and supplies examples of different types of quantitative data that exists in historical and social sciences sources. A section discusses how easily quantitative methods loan themselves to developing critical thinking skills in history and the social sciences.

Employ chapter 1 as an educator to aid your understanding of how quantitative data can be used either centrally or peripherally in your instruction. Familiarize yourself with the various quantitative literacy criteria. Explore the large web sites that are listed within broad data categories such as demographics, economics, and event-related. Read about how to collaborate with the mathematics department if you feel unsure about conducting a quantitative literacy–based lesson. Finally, plan on examining some outstanding university sites that already have quantitative literacy programs in place for history and the social sciences.

Chapter 2 describes how quantitative sources can be presented and displayed in student research assignments and furnishes guidelines for the appropriate use of various types of graphs such as histograms and pie charts. It features guidelines for evaluating data-rich documents. Sets of best practices for displaying specific types of quantitative data and models of correct visual displays of data are included. Refer to this chapter, for example, when advising students about the appropriateness of using a histogram and the correct format for displaying data in tabular form.

Chapters 3 through 5 contain eighty-five historical and social sciences–related Internet sites arranged alphabetically within broad subject headings. A summary of the site supplies background material and highlights of each site's contents followed by four critical thinking skills questions and/ or activities that relate to the primary source. Two briefly annotated subject-related Internet sites follow the questions. These supplemental sites furnish either subject-related background or overview material. In some cases, they may also include additional sources on the same subject. Use the questions for a classroom-based activity to supplement a textbook assignment or for a complete lesson about how to employ quantitative sources as the central part of a research assignment.

SITE SELECTION CRITERIA

Several criteria were used for site selection. The first was to include sites that were related to most standard history and social sciences curricula. This meant searching for sites from a world-wide range of history and the social sciences ranging from the seventeenth to twenty-first centuries. Sometimes it was easy to locate historical and social sciences sources about a particular event or period of history that contained quantitative data either embedded in the text, tabulated, or graphed. Other times, despite extended search efforts, the result was a disappointing zero.

The second criterion was to include sites that students would find exciting, stimulating, and interesting to make it easier to teach critical thinking skills. Thus you will find facts and figures about the 1948 Berlin airlift, the Chernobyl catastrophe, the Dust Bowl, famine in Ireland, 1929 Stock Market crash, and Salem Witch trials in addition to data within large U.S. Civil War databases, census sites, and the National Security Archives. I also deliberately searched for sites that were sponsored by universities, academic libraries, or other reputable think tanks and institutions.

I relied upon the accuracy of their data and graphical presentations. I also thought that they might withstand the vicissitudes of moving, changing their addresses, disappearing, or commercialization in the future. A significant number of sites are census related because they contain significant amounts of valid and reliable quantitative data and because of the stability they represented for future reference.

The final criterion was to have a selection of quantitative sources that reflected the diversity of the world. Unfortunately, this objective was not so easily achieved. Because of language barriers, many sites from Asia, for example, are not available in English. While I found many sites about Africa, finding ones with quantitative data was a challenge. Despite these setbacks, users will find it evident that the Internet still represents a wealth of quantitative sources for future history and social sciences educators to use to teach critical thinking skills.

INTERNET IDIOSYNCRACIES

Although I have endeavored to select resources that will remain on the Internet, there is no way to guarantee that they will. The Internet, as wonderful as it is, is not a stable electronic information resource as is a proprietary database such as Historical Abstracts. It is possible that some Internet addresses will be unresponsive for a variety of technical, personal, or commercial reasons. I have attempted to verify their availability as this book went to press. If an Internet address is inaccessible, refer to the site title and enter the keywords in a search engine such as Google. Perhaps the site may still be retrieved though it may have moved to a new address. Another solution may be to visit the Wayback Machine at the Internet Archive (http://archive.org/web/web.php).

Sometimes another institution is hosting the site and you will be given a new Web address. Another solution may be to wait a month and try again. Some authors or institutions may remove the site entirely when they wish to repair parts of it or make changes. As a last resort, try removing the last part(s) of the URL address and try to connect to the main sponsoring institution. Once there, search for the title of the database if the site has a search engine or browse their set of links to see if it is listed.

A second area for possible problems rests with the directions for using a specific site. The instructions given for selecting a particular page or clicking on a specific link may have become obsolete if a site has been moved or redesigned since this book was published. Again the best solution is to identify the keywords or subject matter of the question and re-explore where or how the site sponsors are allowing users to access it.

REFERENCES

Ayres, I. (2007). *Super-crunchers: Why thinking-by-numbers is the new way to be smart*. New York: Bantam.

Carnevale, A.P., Smith, N., & Strohl, J. (2010, June). "Projection of Jobs and Educational Requirements through 2018." Retrieved from: http://www9.georgetown.edu/grad/gppi/hpi/cew/pdfs/State-LevelAnalysis-web.pdf

Common Core State Standards Initiative. (2012). Retrieved from: http://www.corestandards.org/ELA-Literacy/RH/9-10

Craver, K.W. (1994). *School library media centers in the 21st century changes and challenges*. Westport, CT: Greenwood Press.

Freeland, C. (2012). *Plutocrats: The rise of the new global super-rich and the fall of everyone else*. New York: Penguin Press.

High Growth Industry Profile Information Technology. (2010, March 8). Retrieved from: http://www.doleta.gov/brg/indprof/IT_profile.cfm

Mayer-Schonberger, V., & Cukier, K. (2013). *Big data: A revolution that will transform how we live, work, and think*. New York: Houghton Mifflin.

Paul, R. (1993). *Critical thinking: What every person needs to survive in a rapidly changing world*. Santa Rosa, CA: Foundation for Critical Thinking.

Reich, R. (1991). *The work of nations*. New York: Alfred A. Knopf.

Steen, L.A. (1999). Numeracy: The new literacy for a data-drenched society. *Educational Leadership* 57, 8–13.

Steen, L.A. (2000, Spring). Reading writing, and numeracy. *Liberal Education* 86, 26–37.

Trilling, B., & Fadel, C. (2012). *21st century skills: Learning for life in our times*. San Francisco: Jossey-Bass.

U.S. 21st Century Workforce Commission. (2000, June 1). Retrieved from: http://digitalcommons.ilr.cornell.edu/cgi/viewcontent.cgi?article=1003&context=key_workplace

Wallsten, P. (2003, March 21). Senate plan could double high-skilled worker visas. *Washington Post* A4–A5.

Chapter One

Using Quantitative Sources

AN OVERVIEW OF QUANTITATIVE LITERACY

Historians and social scientists have been publishing articles and books in their respective disciplines that were solely based on quantitative data since the 1970s when mainframe computers at universities gave them the ability to count, total, and compare large series of numbers with minimal error in a relatively short period of time. At the university level, quantitative research expanded into almost every area of history and the social sciences.

Historians and social scientists were able to study voting patterns, the economics of slavery, class structure, and even shed light on the Middle Ages by examining social indicators such as rents, agricultural yields, taxes levied, and population densities (Herlihy, 1972, 20). As more historical and social science sources were published containing data, the ability to interpret, discover patterns, hypothesize, determine correlations, and shed light on causation and change over time was no longer the purview of students in the physical sciences. It also belonged to the world of the historian and social scientist.

When software packages such as IBM SPSS Statistics, SAGE, and SAS were developed, many colleges and universities began to include database development and statistical analysis in their required set of courses for all history and social science majors. Beginning in the 1990s, however, when computers were ubiquitous, information became even more data-based. With a few strokes using spreadsheet software, information that would normally be confined to text could be transformed into sophisticated tables, pie charts, graphs, and histograms.

By the end of the twentieth century, significant numbers of newspaper and periodical articles featured graphics with charts, and graphs that regularly compared prices for similar sized automobiles, evaluated different forms of medical treatments, and displayed current immigration patterns in selected states. The ability to correctly interpret and make an intelligent decision based on this data was assumed on the part of publishers.

Unfortunately, this is a false assumption because studies reveal that only one in ten adults can reliably solve problems that require two or more steps. Moreover, fewer can understand the ramifications of AIDS clinical trials or the implementation of a flat-tax system (Steen, 2004, xvi). About 40 percent of the country's seventeen-year-olds can solve problems including finding 87 percent of 10, or computing the area of a rectangle (Steen, 1990, 215).

Innumeracy also afflicts students at our flagship universities as test scores revealed that even Harvard students experienced a challenge in passing a multiple choice, high school–level data analysis test that was recently a graduation requirement. Nearly 50 percent of the students failed their first attempt at the test even though many of them had passed an AP calculus course. Testers were surprised when many accessed their calculators to find the answer to the question, "What is 10% of 100?" (Steen, 2000, 5–6).

Proponents of quantitative literacy (QL) are not shocked at these findings. Many have backgrounds in different forms of mathematics and have observed and reported how their students have tried to memorize formulas rather than reason their way through a problem because mathematics is not sufficiently context-based. For ten years, beginning in 1980, grants from the Alfred P. Sloan Foundation were designed to centralize mathematics in the liberal arts curriculum and integrate quantitative reasoning skills into humanities-based college courses.

In the mid-1990s, the National Science Foundation's program funded mathematically infused courses on many college campuses with grants (Steen, 2000, 29). In 2001, the National Academy of Sciences instituted a National Forum on Quantitative Literacy that concluded how "QL is largely absent from our current systems of assessment and accountability" (Grawe, 2011, 43). Since that time, the National Numeracy Network was formed to further education that instills quantitative skills across all disciplines and levels. It promotes QL collaboration among students, educators, academic centers, universities, and professional societies and corporations that understand the need for an integration of quantitative reasoning in all subject areas (National Numeracy Network, 2013).

In 2009, a survey of U.S. colleges by the Mathematical Association of America reported that nearly two-thirds of member institutions sponsor a quantitative support center (Schield, 2010, 1). Although the case for QL is evident in low test score results, living in an increasingly data-driven society with additional employment requirements has not produced a standard-based government-sponsored report similar to *A Nation at Risk* that formally documents the dire need for secondary and postsecondary American students to be quantitatively literate. One of the reasons may lie with the definition of quantitative literacy.

DEFINITIONAL PROBLEMS

There is considerable disagreement among scholars and researchers regarding QL terminology, definitions, and characteristics. Terms such as quantitative reasoning and numeracy have been used as synchronous concepts. There are also major differences as to how one defines QL and what characterizes it. Some researchers describe QL as "sophisticated reasoning with elementary mathematics rather than elementary reasoning with sophisticated mathematics" (Grawe, 2011, 42).

Carleton's Quantitative Inquiry, Reasoning, and Knowledge (QuIRK) Initiative states that QL is "the habit of mind to consider both the power and limitations of quantitative evidence in the evaluation, construction, and communication of arguments in public, professional and personal life" (Carleton's Quantitative Inquiry, Reasoning, and Knowledge [QuIRK] Initiative, 2009). In the book *Mathematics and Democracy: The Case for Quantitative Literacy* (Mathematical Association of America, 2001), the National Council on Education and the Disciplines defines it as "contextually appropriate decision-making and interpretation of data" (Jordan and Haines, 2003, 17).

Since QL comprises a complex set of concepts and can be integrated into various academic subjects, it may be important to consider the definition from the perspective of the historian and social scientist. It is clear that historians and social scientists have definitely benefited from applying quantitative methods to their respective disciplines. Quantitative methods have been able to shed light on the extent, for example, that President Andrew Jackson's attitudes and policies towards U.S. banks had upon price levels and employment that affected the boom and bust of the 1830s (Fogel, 1975, 329–330).

Social scientists rely upon quantitative data to examine the accuracy of polls and why they sometimes fail or to investigate which schools seem to be experiencing educational gains compared to other institutions (Steen, 2004, 22). To historians and social scientists, the elements of literacy and numbers have almost become blended since numeracy has become such a staple of life. A number of prominent historians, however, have made the attempt to define this necessary skill for furthering the study of history.

University of California, Los Angeles, historian Theodore Porter defines QL as "an understanding of measurement and calculation as social activities, and of the problems to which they are applied in domains such as economics, society, medicine, and government" (Porter, 1997, 9). Psychology Professor Iddo Gal of the University of Haifa considers QL to be an aggregation of skills, knowledge, beliefs, dispositions, habits of mind, communication capabilities, and problem-solving skills that people need to autonomously engage in and effectively manage in life and at work that involve numbers, quantitative information, or textual information that is based on or has embedded in it some mathematical elements (Gal, 1997, 39).

Although it is obvious that many of these definitions were formulated by scholars to suit the design of their studies and philosophical framework, they do expand on the somewhat amorphous concept of QL, and they also may confuse educators who wish to employ the concepts in their respective disciplines. Steen, in her book *Why Numbers Count*, seems to recommend an eclectic approach to quantitative literacy (Steen, 1977).

Rather than choosing one definition, why not employ a list of definitions that indeed reflect several views of QL? Steen's understanding of QL is that it has become an absolutely essential component of our society. Students who graduate and confidently think that they will never need quantitative skills again do so at significant risk of future underemployment and/or unemployment. QL will be a necessity in home, personal finance, work, testing, parenting, and voting.

Steen defines QL as a "working synthesis of literacy and numeracy that evolves with technology; and shapes and is shaped by society" (Steen, 1997, xvi). While a universal definition of QL would be helpful for measurement and evaluation purposes, it does have a set of characteristics and components that can be applied to history and the social sciences.

QUANTITATIVE LITERACY CRITERIA

Multiple definitions of QL are useful only to an extent. History and social science educators also need a set of criteria by which they can measure the degree to which an assignment is characterized by QL. The following list is adapted from the *Case for Quantitative Literacy Report* by the Mathematical Association of America and the *Valid Assessment of Learning in Undergraduate Education* published by the American Association of Colleges and Universities (2009). Students need to:

- be proficient in basic arithmetic and algebra and the ability to count, calculate, and manipulate quantities
- numerically comprehend and pose questions about the assignment
- locate relevant quantitative evidence to support historical or social sciences questions and problems
- find, collect, or access credible and reliable data to answer historical or social sciences questions

- read and interpret representations of quantitative information such as tables, charts, and graphs
- select the applicable quantitative method to study the question
- explain and justify conclusions made with quantitative information including determining the appropriateness of the conclusion
- derive the correct analysis based upon the selected data
- understand the difference between correlation and causality
- have strategies for making decisions in the face of uncertainty and incomplete data
- translate the findings to answer the question(s) at issue
- acknowledge the limitations of the numerical method utilized
- incorporate quantitative measures of uncertainty in understanding assertions, such as those found in popular media
- produce basic numerical and graphical summaries of data
- communicate quantitative information in written or graphical forms
- disseminate and/or present the numerical data in proper formats
- have a more positive feeling about the use of quantitative information and be more disposed towards using it (Grawe and Rutz, 2009, 4; Wolfe, 2010, 449).

With these general components in mind, it is important to know what types of learning activities are conducive to producing quantitative thinkers. Most empirical and qualitative research suggest that QL is related to reading, mathematics, and writing. All of these activities are constantly employed in the study of history and the social sciences. The biggest challenge facing educators at all levels, however, is how to integrate each skill into different disciplines.

QUANTITATIVE LITERACY RESEARCH RESULTS

Proponents of QL are usually members of the mathematics department. They consider QL to be a distinct form of mathematics that does not require sophisticated mathematical skills as outlined in the assessment skills in the previous section. QL assessment has two requirements, however, that have remained challenges to meet. The concepts and skills cannot be totally taught by the members of mathematics departments. The skills must be integrated into courses in the humanities as well as the physical sciences.

QL advocates believe that "the test of numeracy, as of any literacy, is whether a person naturally uses appropriate skills in many different contexts" (Steen, 2001, 6). In the past decades, a person's second academic hurdle is overcoming the "mathphobia" that exists within departments in the humanities and social sciences, as noted in the math anxiety books written by

Tobias (Tobias, 12). This is why some of QL assessment research employs qualitative and quantitative methods and is sometimes confined to assessments completed with students only within the mathematics department.

As the need for context-related QL to be taught grows, more QL proponents are designing valid and reliable assessments of QL in an attempt to develop a standardized, normed evaluation. Wellesley College, for example, has been administering a school-based quantitative reasoning assessment to incoming students for the past ten years to determine whether students need a remedial course before tackling courses that entail math, logic, and basic statistics. Unfortunately, the test does not measure whether the students have the ability to apply quantitative reasoning skills outside of a mathematics class.

Dartmouth College has developed a "Mathematics Attitude Survey" (MAS) that measures students' attitudes and perceived mathematical confidence and ability. The Dartmouth MAS instrument is being recommended for post-change measurement and evaluation after students take a QL course. James Madison University administers a quantitative reasoning test after students have completed their general mathematics requirement. It is a twenty-six-item computerized multiple choice test that measures and evaluates whether students were able to graphically represent data and understand the correct evidence to establish causation.

The American Association of Colleges and Universities has created a fourteen-item QL rubric that's designed to assess various components of QL. This rubric can assist faculty members who wish to assess their QL efforts in the classroom (Taylor, 2009, 2–3). Carleton College has developed an outstanding example of integrating QL skills into the various academic disciplines and has established a web site called the Quantitative Inquiry, Reasoning, Knowledge Initiative (QUIRK). The site is filled with curricular activities, workshop materials, and assessment rubric and guidelines for teaching quantitative reasoning within the context of other disciplines.

In 2009, Professor Nathan Grawe and his co-authors published the results of a rubric that they developed to test the extent of quantitative reasoning in a written argument. The test group of 207 student papers were submitted and graded by faculty and readers from natural science, social science, and arts and literature departments. Student papers were assessed to determine whether quantitative reasoning was either a central or peripheral part of their papers as well as their use of appropriate numerical evidence.

This assessment is the first one that faculty can use to measure and evaluate the use of quantitative reasoning in context of a humanities or physical science course. It can easily be adopted as a pre- and post-measure for assessing the value of teaching a course in QL prior to selected or advanced courses in the humanities at the high school or undergraduate level (Grawe, 2010, 3–6).

APPLYING QUANTITATIVE LITERACY SKILLS TO THE STUDY OF HISTORY AND THE SOCIAL SCIENCES

The implications of these findings for history and social science educators are exciting. Secondary schools offer a natural setting in which to employ quantitative reasoning skills with history and social science students. It also serves as an excellent laboratory for applying various methods and techniques of quantitative reasoning instruction. History and social science educators are fortunate that their subjects loan themselves to developing quantitative reasoning skills. Historical and social science data can be employed as the central or peripheral part of student assignments. The study of history and the social sciences is predisposed to either approach.

The social sciences, including history, can be studied three ways, and all provide the opportunity to introduce quantitative reasoning skills that give students the means to determine patterns, draw inferences, manipulate data, and establish cause and effect or change over time. The narrative approach looks at what specific people have done, said, and thought in the past. Historians who approach the discipline from a biographical perspective attempt to reconstruct the life, thoughts, and times of individuals who actually lived in the past. Finding a database of four thousand people who were accused of witchcraft in the sixteenth through eighteenth centuries is a historical goldmine for shedding light on the types of people who were most likely to be accused of witchcraft. There are numerous historical quantitative questions that can be generated from such an extensive database.

The sociological school of history analyzes human beings in their social aspects both past and present (Cantor and Schneider, 1968, 17). Manipulating the variables at the *Historical Census Data Browser* site, for example, can produce demographic evidence of the extent of slavery in U.S. northern versus southern states. Narrative history can take one of four approaches: political-institutional, intellectual, economic, or cultural. Political-institutional history focuses on what people have said, thought, and done in government and law. A search of the Chernobyl Catastrophe site, for example, provides data about how the Soviet government responded to the explosion of their nuclear reactor that released huge amounts of radiation into the atmosphere, contaminating people and the environment.

Economic historians and social scientists research how people are making or have made a living and maintain their surroundings. Employing a site about Bosnia's civil war (stathis.research.yale.edu/documents/Bosnia.pdf) that provides data showing the pre-war income per capita and unemployment rates can be used by students to analyze how these factors may have contributed to the subsequent war that splintered Yugoslavia. Some historians and social scientists believe that this form of research is the main vehicle for revealing human thought and action.

Cultural historians and social scientists are often thought as generalists. A cultural researcher in history and the social sciences explores the development of ideas in their social, political, and economic context (Cantor and Schneider, 1968, 17–21). Data at the Cold War Air Defense site about the accumulation of U.S. and U.S.S.R. nuclear weapons can be analyzed by students to draw inferences about the culture of the Cold War during the 1950s (Cold War Air Defense, 2010).

The study of history as the biography of important women and men is also dimensional in scope. One school of the social sciences holds that the actions of men and women in the past can and should be examined in terms of modern psychological theories and concepts. Whereas a second school of thought believes that men's and women's lives can only be studied in light of the prevailing psychological concepts, beliefs, and theories of their era. Researching the life of former President Lyndon Johnson and discovering how economically deprived he was as a child can provide significant insight on his decision to declare war on poverty in America with the establishment of various government-sponsored anti-poverty programs.

The social sciences study human beings in their past and present social aspects. Sociology is also divided into schools of thought. It explores the characteristics and actions of a distinct society, group, or community and compares similar patterns found in all or several societies. Students, for example, who use the data at the African Activist Archive (n.d.) will find statistics showing a pattern of escalation on the part of black South Africans to demand their freedom and civil rights from the apartheid government that is consistent with other human rights movements in the past and present day.

Despite the complexity of social science schools of thought, students still need to find evidence about the past or present and evaluate its significance to a particular area of study. The social sciences are not just about fact collection. They are also about amassing appropriate evidence to enable a student to establish casual relationships and change over time that will shed light on the hows and whys of history and the social sciences (Cantor and Schneider, 1968, 17–22).

To be able to provide quantitative evidence on the hows and whys of the social sciences requires two elements: (1) access to valid and reliable Internet sites containing quantitative data in history and the social sciences, and (2) the motivation by history and social science educators to introduce students to these much neglected sources of evidence.

When students rely upon a secondary source, usually a history textbook, as their basic source, they do not have to employ many of the quantitative skills that are set forth in the Common Core State Standards Initiatives that include the ability to "integrate quantitative or technical analysis (e.g. charts, research data) with qualitative analysis and analyze quantitative information to address a question or solve a problem" (Common Core State Standards Initiatives, 2012).

Using quantitative evidence is not much different from using primary text sources. Quantitative evidence provides an opportunity for students to build the following competencies that are cited in David Kobrin's (1996) book *Beyond the Textbook: Teaching History Using Documents and Primary Sources*, and the Common Core State Standards for History and Social Studies Students in Grades 9–12. Students must be able to:

- Explore different ideas, think divergently, take risks, and express opinions. These generalities include the ability to speculate, infer, hypothesize, entertain alternative scenarios, pose questions, make predictions, and think metaphorically.
- Examine multiple possibilities of meaning and determine the cultural and psychological nuances and complexities in a text.
- Understand the importance of context and perspective in a source and be able to examine internal and external evidence to determine its validity.
- Discern the main ideas in a historical or social science source.
- Make connections between the source and one's own ideas, experiences, and knowledge.
- Make generalizations that are supported by historical and social science evidence.
- Discern themes and patterns in a set of primary sources.
- Communicate one's ideas clearly and persuasively in oral and written communication.
- Collaborate with peers in group interaction assignments.

Quantitative reasoning in history and the social sciences cannot be taught all at once. It can be helpful, however, to devise assignments that highlight or reinforce specific skills such as locating relevant quantitative evidence: to support historical or social sciences questions and problems; to find, collect, or access credible and reliable data to answer historical or social sciences questions; to read and interpret representations of quantitative information such as tables, charts, and graphs; and to select the applicable quantitative method to study the question at hand. What is also important is to create assignments that repetitively foster these skills so that students eventually internalize them for all types of future work.

WHAT ARE QUANTITATIVE SOURCES?

For analysis purposes, there are two types of quantitative sources: categorical data and numeric data. Within each of these types there are two subgroups.

Categorical data contain nominal data that are not ordered in any way. This data might be discovered in a text, for example, that list the occupations, gender, race, religion, or nationalities of a group of people. The second subclass within categorical data comprises ordinal data, which rank something in order.

Examples of this type of data might include someone's economic or social classification that one might encounter in an article about the class system in the Middle Ages which lists the number of vassals, serfs, etc. Numeric data comprise interval data that measure the range or distance between meaningful values. Examples of interval data might include years, dollars, and test scores. Ratio data feature a scale of measurement where the differences between data can be counted and proportions allotted. Examples of ratio data allow one to compute that a sixteen-year-old is four times as old as a four-year-old (Hudson, 2000, 53–55).

Categorical data loan themselves to descriptive statistics that allow students to present quantitative sources in the form of tables and charts or summarize into percentages. Numeric data are susceptible to inferential statistics and may require students to have more knowledge of statistics than is necessary to respond to the questions about the various quantitative sources cited in this book.

QUANTITATIVE CLASSIFICATION

Quantitative sources span a vast amount of time and materials and are highly diversified in character. They include numbers displayed within text and in tables, graphs, charts, maps, iconic representation, and diagrams. They consist of just about everything that one can count: taxes, immigration, visas, applications, and questionnaire forms are possible sources as well as information sheets, timetables, price lists, catalogs, and programs. Certificates, diplomas, contracts, and advertisements can also be valuable quantitative references (De Lange, 2003, 76).

Although the statistical displays that students encounter daily on the Internet are the usual frame of reference for quantitative sources, at least one hundred thousand of them dating from the second and seventh Christian centuries have been digitized and are available to scholars. What are they? Years ago, the inscriptions on tombs frequently recorded the sex and age of the deceased and sometimes her/his accomplishments in life. This data can now be used to estimate mortality rates and life expectancies within an ancient society.

During the time of the Carolingian empire, fifty thousand acts showing property transactions have survived as sources that can be used to study the power of the Catholic church during from 750 A.D. These valuable sources give history and social science students the means to expand their views of a problem, shed light on possible cause and effect, or provide insight about change over time (Herlihy, 1972, 18–19).

The range of quantitative sources is so broad that classifying them is the only way to impose order on such a chaotic assortment of materials. For the sake of organization and improving student search results, the following annotated, data-rich sites within broad divisions may be illustrative and helpful.

Demographic Data

This type of data describes populations and usually includes specific numbers concerning population size and growth, age, sex, race, and household and family structure.

Demographic Data Source Examples

American FactFinder (n.d.): Features census data from the 1990 and 2000 censuses and annual population estimates. Students can enter specific data and produce their own tables and maps.

Historical Census Browser (2007): Contains summary-level census data from 1790 to 1960 that describes the economy and population from each census time period. This database provides table and graph creation.

Earthtrends—World Resources Institute (n.d.): Furnishes data related to economic and environmental development and social trends throughout the world. This site features sub-links for population, health, and the environment.

UN Statistics (2013): Contains demographic, economic, and other types of data about every UN member country, including a set of related international data links.

Vision of Britain through Time (2009): Supplies quantitative data about 408 local government areas from every census from 1801 through 2001. This site is replete with charts, graphs, and maps that display periods of employment and poverty, housing patterns, and social strata.

Economic Data

This type of data provides information about businesses, industries, economies, and the labor force. Figures about people concerning poverty, households, and family composition are also included.

Economic Data Source Examples

Children's Defense Fund (2012): Gives facts and summary statistics for issues related to children's welfare including child care, gun violence against children, federal funding of education for children, population, and poverty levels.

    China Data Center (n.d.): Sponsored by the University of Michigan, this site integrates historical, social, and natural science data within a geographic information system. It also includes data and statistics from the 2000 Chinese census.

    Eurostat (2013): Provides a wealth of statistics about the demographics, economies, and environment of the European Union. Data are grouped into easily accessible themes under headings such as "Population and Social Conditions" and "Economy and Finance." This site also features tables and an advanced query system for individualized data downloads.

    Global Statistics World Community Grid (2013): Contains student-friendly demographic and economic statistics about regions, provinces, countries, and cities of the world. The country pages contain related links for locating additional statistics.

    NationMaster: Where Stats Come Alive (2013): This enormous database gives students an easy way to graphically compare countries regarding more than 1,180 statistics including subjects such as literacy, religious affiliation, poverty, and more. It also furnishes map and graph-making capabilities.

Social and Behavioral Data

This type of data encompass a broad range of subjects including education, crime, justice, religion, sexual behavior, and substance abuse. Opinion poll and other questionnaire type data are also part of this section.

Social and Behavioral Data Source Examples

Bureau of Justice Statistics (2013): Contains national statistics about crime and victims, criminal offenders, the courts and sentencing, types of crimes, combating crime, and the functioning of various justice systems at all levels.

    Harris Vault (2013): This polling site is searchable back to 1970 about issues including politics, science and technology, healthcare, foreign affairs, social and lifestyle issues, and sports. It is a valuable source of data for students who wish to study an aspect of cultural history.

    NCAA Sports Statistics (2013): Sports are the great American pastime, and this site furnishes statistics regarding basketball, football, volleyball, swimming, and more. It is also searchable by player/coach and team name.

Records also exist for women's participation in basketball, volleyball, gymnastics, soccer, and cross-country.

South African Data Archive (n.d.): This site provides linkage to different government- and university-sponsored sites that contain data about substance abuse, AIDS, crime, poverty, and political perceptions and attitudes. Click on the humanities link to access historical sites with information about South Africa's apartheid period.

Statistical Materials for Learning about Japan (2012): Students can click on the English version of this site to find statistics about population, crime, housing and land, family budget, and education. World history students can click on the "long-term statistics" link to retrieve data back to 1868.

Event-Related Data

This type of data provides quantitative information in various formats about specific historical or social sciences–related occurrences that altered history and/or affected lives.

Event-Related Data Source Examples

The Chernobyl Catastrophe: Consequences on Human Health (2006): Sponsored by Greenpeace, this site contains data about death rates, cancer rates, and government compensation involving the meltdown of nuclear reactor number four at the Chernobyl Atomic Energy Station in the Ukraine in 1986.

The History of the Present State of the Ottoman Empire (Rycaut, 1682): The statistics contained in this online book, which was published in 1665, contain one of the few existing sources about the military and naval strength and the daily functioning of the Ottoman Empire during the seventeenth century.

The Nanking Massacre Project (2008): Provides damage data documents from Yale University about the terrible World War II atrocities committed by the Japanese against the Chinese in the city of Nanking in 1937.

The Peter G. Peterson Foundation (2013): Created in 2008 to publicize the danger of the U.S. debt, this site is replete with charts, statistics, and financial figures. Some of the data go back to the nineteenth century.

Triangle Shirtwaist Factory Fire (2013): Harvard University hosts four volumes titled "Report of the Committee" that investigated the results of the fire in a shirtwaist factory that killed 146 workers on March 25, 1911.

QUANTITATIVE SOURCE CAVEATS

Quantitative sources may be subjective, polemical, and illustrative of one opinion or have a limited perspective even though they are in the form of numbers. Suppose that in the year 2500, historians find statistics published by the National Rifle Association, a right to life group, or the Hemlock Society. It is likely that the data would reflect the point of view of the group that published them. It is critical that students must obtain sufficient background material about all data sources so that they can evaluate them for potential bias.

QUANTITATIVE SOURCE PREPARATIONS

Employing quantitative sources in a history or social sciences curriculum that is highly content-structured and prescheduled requires some classroom planning and management skills. Here are some considerations for ensuring a successful quantitative resource–based unit. Answer the following questions: (1) Will the activity be instructor designed, adopted, or adapted from a selected QL site? (2) Will you have individual, group, or entire class participation? (3) What type of product/presentation do you wish students to complete to measure their achievement level with quantitative sources?

INSTRUCTOR-DESIGNED QUANTITATIVE LITERACY CURRICULUM ACTIVITIES

Quantitative sources can be used in a variety of ways in the classroom. Employing them for curriculum-based activities creates an atmosphere where critical thinking skills can easily be integrated into learning and where the instructor serves as a guide rather than as the sole source of information and knowledge. Finding quantitative sources for a specific resource-based unit, however, can sometimes be problematic.

While there are hundreds of large databases containing statistics, such as American Factfinder and Global Statistics, they do not offer the opportunity to place a lesson within context of the syllabus. Searching for context-related quantitative sources is somewhat challenging but also immensely satisfying because the activity being taught is usually more relevant and interesting to the students. If you are a history or social sciences educator, seek the assistance of a librarian in finding sources or better still, combine their searching skills with your subject-based skills.

Google is a likely place to start not only because of the power of its algorithms but also because of its additional free databases Google Books and Google Scholar. *The History of the Present State of the Ottoman Empire* is an example of a book that is no longer under copyright protection and is available in full text in Google Books. Scrolling through the pages produces lists and tables of data about the military, political, and social conditions of the Ottoman Empire in the seventeenth century. Google scholar features scholarly articles, web sites, and reports from many disciplines.

Use the general search first by entering content-related keywords followed by the words "statistics," "data," or "numbers." See the following example:

> Google Scholar: online student dropouts + statistics
> online student dropouts + data
> online student dropout + numbers

When you locate an article or report that seems to match the search terms, read the abstract, highlight additional specific search terms, and click on the Google Scholar Advanced Search. This search box provides limiting features so one can search within a specific date range and add additional keywords. While many of the articles may be pay-per-view, some are free and downloadable. Articles that are proprietary can usually be located in subject-specific databases that are available on almost any school or public library web site.

Almost all secondary school and public libraries offer commercial databases such as EBSCOhost (large periodicals database) and SIRS that are easily searched using similar word syntaxes. The latter two are prime for locating context-related data to introduce quantitative skills to classes in the social sciences. For history students, databases such as JSTOR and Project Muse would serve similar purposes.

QUANTITATIVE LITERACY CURRICULUM ACTIVITIES SITES

While many history and social science educators might wish to locate their own quantitative sources and create questions about them, there are several excellent web sites with QL activities that are well worth a visit prior to reinventing the wheel. The first is a site from George Mason University titled *History Matters* (2013). It is more than robust for it features not only hundreds of annotated links to quantitative sources in U.S. history but also sequenced lesson plans for working with data. After mining this site for future quantitative resources for student use, visit "Making Sense of Numbers" (http://historymatters.gmu.edu/mse/numbers/index.html).

This QL tutorial for history educators is graduated. If you decide to use it with students, you will need to know their level of QL. Some of George Mason's studies utilize grade eight mathematical operations such as addition, subtraction, multiplication, and division. Other parts of the tutorial employ advanced inferential statistical techniques that probably require high school and undergraduate students to have taken a statistics course. All of the lessons use primary source quantitative data from valid U.S. historical sources, making this site extremely applicable for U.S. history classes. The tutorial lends itself to individual, small group or class size work and participation.

The second site worth exploring is QUIRK, hosted by Carleton College. This site provides a philosophical argument for the need for QL in every subject area. History and social science educators will find links that define QL along with outstanding curricular materials. If you are a social science educator, you may find more lesson plans about political science, economics, and sociology than for history for each curricular activity. There is a similar range of difficulty, with each site depending upon the mathematical skills of the user.

This site excels in supplying all the rudiments for introducing quantitative reasoning into non-mathematical assignments. It delivers a foundation in the basic components with excellent final product examples of quantitative writing in fields such as economics and political science. Although this site lacks a tutorial similar to George Mason University's that could be used with little preparation on the part of the instructor for the entire class, it provides an outstanding database of quantitative reasoning writing that students can refer to when they are working on any future QL assignment.

Carleton College also hosts the National Numeracy Network (http://serc.carleton.edu/nnn/teaching/activities.html), which continues to compile curricular activities, articles, and help aids for teaching QL. The site provides the latest news about how to integrate QL skills into various academic disciplines in addition to how-to links about teaching with data and models. In referencing lesson plans, this site is unique.

It has isolated the individual quantitative skills such as estimation or fractions and ratios in each lesson plan so that QL users can link only to those curricular activities that contain that specific mathematical function or level. Many of the lesson plans provide either historical or social sciences data and are graded for high school and upwards. This site would be excellent for history and social science educators who want to use a graduated mathematical approach to introducing QL assignments into their curricula.

Dartmouth College (http://www.math.dartmouth.edu/~mqed/eBookshelf/index.php) maintains a site titled *The Center for Mathematics and Quantitative Education* that also fosters the acquisition of quantitative skills throughout their curriculum. In addition to providing dozens of downloadable curricular activities in history, business and economics, and health, Dartmouth offers entire learning modules that provide instruction about various mathematical skills required for QL such as data analysis and discrete math.

Their units are artfully arranged in an "Electronic Bookshelf" that links to displayed subject categories. For secondary history and social science educators, Dartmouth sponsors a set of lessons plans called "Little Bookshelf" that includes a multitude of QL units for students in grades six to twelve (Center for Mathematics and Quantitative Electronic Bookshelf at Dartmouth, n.d.). Each one of their learning modules contains downloadable copies of the necessary data, or it can be easily requested from the instructor.

QUANTITATIVE INSTRUCTIONAL STRATEGIES

When Professor Grawe was developing a rubric to assess papers written using various elements of QL, he assigned a quality score based on whether components of numerical evidence were used either peripherally or centrally in the paper (Grawe, 2010, 6). Quantitative sources can be used in a variety of ways in the classroom. They can be analyzed on several levels and differences in students' competencies, and interests can be channeled to stimulate class discussions and other quantitative reasoning activities.

Here are two suggested approaches for using the quantitative sources found in chapter 3 or for using ones that you have found on the Internet, in books, or in area archives. You will encounter examples of both these approaches when you peruse the questions posed for each web site in chapter 3.

Peripheral Approach

This approach uses numerical evidence to position the main theme of the paper in an insightful and effective manner. The student makes appropriate comparisons where needed to place the data within the relevant context. This assignment or activity may use quantitative sources as a sole basis for the paper but relies upon other textual sources as well.

Central Approach

In a central approach, the use of numerical evidence is used throughout the paper. The interpretation of the quantitative evidence is correct and complete considering all of the available information. There are no errors, for example, involving statistical analysis between correlation and causation.

Central versus Peripheral

When history and social science educators decide to introduce QL skills into an aspect of their curriculum, it is important not to feel as if one is being remiss if students insert quantitative data only peripherally into their assignments. It has long been observed that most students in the humanities, especially at the secondary and undergraduate levels, are math-averse. Years ago, the British initiated the Cockcroft Commission to learn about how people used mathematics in their daily lives and occupations. They chose to inter-view people rather than administer math-related tests.

Interviewers quickly learned how math-phobic their respondents were when more than half of those solicited refused to be interviewed for the study. Further survey research revealed that many interviewees, when con-fronted with simple mathematical problems, exhibited agitation, fear, and guilt. A second facet of the study uncovered that those who needed to rely upon occupation-mandated mathematics achieved their results by relying on co-workers to pass on various tricks and methods that had little connection with school-based mathematics (Steen, 1990, 215).

Overcoming this type of math anxiety is not going to occur overnight. Students may even be resistant to the introduction of any quantitative reason-ing skills at first because they believe that humanities courses should be totally text-based. If the social science or history course is an elective, the absence of any form of mathematics may have been one of the students' motivating factors for selecting it.

Plan to move incrementally so that the majority of the students experience success and their confidence level increases. Aim for students to be able to discuss data that's embedded in a text or displayed in a table so that it feels as natural to them as it does to discuss the main text-based issues. Be on the alert for students who grasp the application of quantitative reasoning to histo-ry and the social sciences more easily. Target them for work on an assign-ment that employs a central approach and uses quantitative data as complete evidence in support of a thesis.

TEAM UP AND PUBLICIZE IT

Secondary and college-level educators constantly attend discipline-related conferences, faculty meetings, and academic senate and committee meetings. At least one of them regularly features a speaker who extols the need for more interdisciplinary work. Usually, there is the official nodding of heads in agreement, the meeting adjourns, and everyone returns to their insular work in their respective departments. The need for QL is so urgent in the United States that there could not be a better time to establish coordination with history, social studies, and mathematics departments.

Start out with a consultation. If you, as a history or social studies educa-tor, do not feel comfortable introducing quantitative reasoning skills into a course, seek the assistance of someone in the mathematics department. Per-haps that person can teach the part that you feel uncomfortable with or read over a proposed curriculum activity for any egregious mathematical errors before it is presented. Many academic institutions provide grants for summer work. Apply for and write a grant for one resource-based unit that incorporates quantitative data into a humanities course. Share it with other members of both departments, present the results at a convention, post it on the Internet, and create more of them.

QUANTITATIVE LITERACY ASSESSMENT RUBRIC

With the passage of the No Child Left Behind Act in 2001, the United States has become obsessed with assessments. While assessments are necessary to measure progress and achievement and to advance students to the next level, QL does not lend itself to a multiple choice type of measurement that permeates so many aspects of the current curriculum. It is a form of numeracy that by its very ecumenical nature requires integration into other subjects such as history and the social sciences.

The Association of American Colleges and Universities has declared QL "to be 'a habit of mind,' competency and comfort in working with numerical data." To that purpose they have developed a Quantitative Literacy Value Rubric that history and social science educators may wish to use to assess the success of any future project. It can also be employed when designing a curriculum activity as a checklist to determine if all the objectives that history and social science educators wish to include are present. This rubric is available at http://www.aacu.org/value/rubrics/pdf/QuantitativeLiteracy.pdf.

REFERENCES

African Activist Archive. (n.d.). Retrieved from: http://africanactivist.msu.edu/

American FactFinder. (n.d.). Retrieved from: http://factfinder2.census.gov/

Association of American Colleges and Universities. (2009). *VALUE: Valid Assessment of Learning in Undergraduate Education*. Retrieved from: http://www.aacu.org/value/metarubrics.cfm

Bureau of Justice Statistics. (2013). Retrieved from: http://www.bjs.gov/

Cantor, N., and Schneider, R.I. (1968). *How to study history*. New York: Thomas Y. Crowell.

Carleton's Quantitative Inquiry, Reasoning, and Knowledge (QUIRK) Initiative. (2009, July). Retrieved from: http://serc.carleton.edu/quirk/index.html

Center for Mathematics and Quantitative Electronic Bookshelf at Dartmouth. (n.d.). Retrieved from: http://www.math.dartmouth.edu/~mqed/eBookshelf/

The Chernobyl Catastrophe: Consequences on Human Health. (2006). Retrieved from: http://www.greenpeace.org/international/Global/international/planet-2/report/2006/4/chernobyl-healthreport.pdf)

Children's Defense Fund. (2012). Retrieved from: http://www.childrensdefense.org/

China Data Center. (n.d.). Retrieved from: http://chinadatacenter.org/

Cold War Air Defense Relied Upon Widespread Dispersal of Nuclear Weapons. (2010, November 16). Retrieved from: www.gwu.edu/~nsarchiv/nukevault/ebb332/

Common Core State Standards Initiative. (2012). Retrieved from: http://www.corestandards.org/ELA-Literacy

De Lange, J. (2003). Mathematics for literacy. In: B. Madison and L.A. Steen (eds.), *Quantitative literacy: Why numeracy matters for schools and colleges (pp. 75–89)*. Princeton, NJ: National Council on Education and the Disciplines.

Earthtrends. (n.d.) Retrieved from: http://www.wri.org/project/earthtrends/

EuroStat. European Commission. (2013, August 11). Retrieved from: http://ec.europa.eu/euros-tat
Fogel, R.W. (1975, April). The limits of quantitative methods in history. *American Historical Review* 80, 329–349.
Gal, I. (1997). Numeracy: Imperatives of a forgotten goal. In: L.A. Steen (ed.) *Why numbers count* (pp. 36–44). New York: College Entrance Examination Board.
Global Statistics World Community Grid. (2013, November 8). Retrieved from: http://www.worldcommunitygrid.org/stat/viewGlobal.do
Grawe, 2009
Grawe, N. (2011, Spring). Beyond math skills: Measuring quantitative reading in context. *New Directions for Institutional Research* 149, 41–52.
Grawe, N.D., & Rutz, C.A. (2008). Integration with writing programs: A strategy for quantitative reasoning program development, *Numeracy* 2(2), 1–18.
Grawe, N.D., et al. (2010). A rubric for assessing quantitative reasoning in written arguments. *Numeracy* 3(1), 1–21.
Harris Vault. (2013). Retrieved from: http://www.harrisinteractive.com/Insights/Harris-Vault.aspx
Herlihy, D. (1972). Quantification and the middle ages. In V.R. Lorwin & J.M. Price (eds.), *The dimensions of the past* (pp. 13–51). New Haven, CT: Yale University Press.
Historical Census Browser. (2007). University of Virginia. Retrieved from: http://mapserver.lib.virginia.edu/
History Matters. (2013). George Mason University. Retrieved from: http://historymatters.gmu.edu/mse/numbers/question4.html
Hudson, P. (2000). *History by numbers an introduction to quantitative approaches*. New York: Oxford University Press.
Jordan, J., & Haines, B. (2003, summer). Fostering quantitative literacy clarifying goals: Assessing student progress. *Peer Review* 5, 16–19.
Kalyvas, S., & Sambanis, N. Bosnia's civil war origins and violence dynamics. In P. Collier and N. Sambanis (eds.) Understanding civil war evidence and analysis (pp. 191–222). Washington, DC: The World Bank. Retrieved from: stathis.research.yale.edu/documents/Bosnia.pdf
Kobrin, D. (1996). *Beyond the textbook: Teaching history using documents and primary sources*. Portsmouth, NH: Heineman.
Mathematical Association of America. (2001). *The case for quantitative literacy*. Retrieved from: http://www.maa.org/ql/001-22.pdf
The Nanking Massacre Project. (2008). Retrieved from: www.library.yale.edu/div/Nanking/
National Numeracy Network. (2013). Retrieved from: http://serc.carleton.edu/nnn/index.html
NationMaster: Where Statistics Come Alive. (2013). Retrieved from: http://www.nationmaster.com/
NCAA Sports Statistics. (2013). Retrieved from: http://www.ncaa.org/wps/wcm/connect/public/NCAA/.../Stats/index.html
The Peter G. Peterson Foundation. (2013). Retrieved from: www.pgpf.org/
Porter, T.M. (1997). The triumph of numbers: Civic implications of quantitative literacy. In L.A. Steen (ed.), *Why numbers count* (pp. 1–10). NY: College Entrance Examination Board.
Rycaut, P. (1682). *The history of the present state of the ottoman empire*. Retrieved from: http://books.google.com/books/about/The_History_of_the_Present_State_of_the.html?id=KKMuTmW98DEC
Schield, M. (2010). Quantitative graduation rates at U.S. four-year volleges. Retrieved from: http://wwww.citeseerx.ist.psu.edu/viewdoc/download?doi=10.1.1.158
South African Data Archive. (n.d.). Retrieved from: http://sada.nrf.ac.za/
Statistical Materials for Learning about Japan. (2012) Retrieved from: http://rnavi.ndl.go.jp/research_guide/statistical-materials-for-learning-about-japan/
Steen, L.A. (ed.). (1977). *Why numbers count: quantitative literacy for tomorrow's America*. New York: The College Board.
Steen, L.A. (1990, Spring). Numeracy. *Daedalus* 119, 211–231.
Steen, L.A. (2000, Spring). Reading, writing, and numeracy. *Liberal Education* 86, 26–37.

Steen, L.A. (ed.). (2001). *Mathematics and democracy: The case for quantitative literacy.* Washington, DC: Woodrow Wilson Fellowship Foundation. Retrieved from: http://www.maa.org/ql/mathanddemocracy.html

Steen, L.A. (2004). *Achieving quantitative literacy: An urgent challenge for higher education.* Washington, DC: Mathematical Association of America.

Taylor, C.H. (2009). Assessing quantitative reasoning. *Numeracy* 2 (2), 1–5.

Tobias, S. (1978). *Overcoming math anxiety.* Boston: Houghton Mifflin.

Tobias, S. (1987). *Succeed with math: Every student's guide to conquering math anxiety.* New York: The College Board.

Triangle Shirtwaist Factory Fire. (2013). New York State Investigating Commission. Retrieved from: http://ocp.hul.harvard.edu/ww/nysfic.html

UN Statistics. (2013). Retrieved from: http://unstats.un.org/

Vision of Britain through Time. (2009). Retrieved from: http://www.visionofbritain.org.uk/

Wolfe, J. (2010). Rhetorical numbers: A case for quantitative writing in the composition classroom. *College Composition and Communication* 61(3), 434–457.

Chapter Two

Interpreting, Displaying, and Visualizing Data

Interpreting data requires simply locating the most relevant quantitative information to a historical or social science–related question, making mathematically correct comparisons among the data, and drawing the appropriate conclusions from the analysis. Most of the data created by students or found within social sciences and historical sources are in the form of percentages, ratios, and averages (Klass, 2012, xiv).

There are some guidelines, however, that may assist students as they examine or design their own displays of data. While not all of them apply to every type of source, they do raise necessary critical thinking questions when students are involved in finding and selecting quantitative sources or creating their own data displays from data-filled documents.

- **Historical context:** Historical context is an important variable when interpreting data. Students need to have background knowledge about a statistic to place it within an analysis framework. How has this statistic changed over time? Is the data different from previous trends? Have these statistics been collected for an extended period of time? Are the data relevant to the issues that I am addressing in the assignment?
- **Geographical:** Is the data different or similar to other comparable geographic areas?
- **Demographic:** How does the value of the data compare to the entire population or number in the problem? Receiving two million ballots after ten million pre-voting ballots were distributed does not permit one to conclude how one-fifth of the total population would actually vote.
- **Rate/percentages:** What does the percentage difference signify with observable data such as people, population, and economics? A 200 percent

increase in AIDS cases may be alarming, but it could only reflect an increase in diagnosed cases from ten in the first year to thirty in the second.

- **Supplementary data:** Do the data provide the main impetus for the assignment, or does the data need to be supported with other social science/ historical evidence?
- **Data limitations:** Have the authors of the data made faulty assumptions or drawn conclusions errantly based on the data?
- **Comparison correctness:** Have the appropriate comparisons been made with the available data? For example, comparing the number of deaths from pneumonia from fifty years ago without adjusting for the increase in population will produce a faulty conclusion.
- **Omission/selection:** Is there a source of data that should have been included? Have the authors selected only data that would support a specific argument or point of view?
- **Graphic displays:** Is the type of data display appropriate to the statistics? For instance, is a pie chart an appropriate way to show the percentage of Catholics versus Muslims and Protestants who obtain divorces? Is the integrity of the data maintained, or have the graphic designers chosen to augment a portion of the data with unusual color or patterns?
- **Survey reliance:** Survey responses are dependent upon how the questions are posed. Questions can be leading, biased, or selective. The response size can also be limited. Asking one hundred people if they believe in the death penalty is not a sufficient number to formulate future government policies regarding capital punishment. While these types of questions can be an interesting source of data for cultural history students, total reliance on the results to establish cause and effect or change over time is limited.
- **Statistical terms:** For history and social science students, statistics are usually used to support associations or change over time. Although statistical analysis can establish mathematically significant relationships between variables that dispel the likelihood of chance, it is still a leap of historical faith to state cause and effect with mathematical certainty. In history and the social sciences, students need to be more circumspect with their statistical assumptions and conclusions. Contributory factors always need to be acknowledged.
- **Definitions:** How someone or something is defined can affect one's statistical interpretation. The U.S. Census Bureau (n.d.) makes a distinction between cities and urbanized areas for analysis purposes, and confusing these terms can change the meaning of the data.
- **Unsupported conclusions:** Drawing conclusions from data that are not fully supported by it is one of the most common errors when relying on statistical evidence. While there may be a correlation, for example, between life expectancy at birth and infant mortality rate, stating that there is

a direct cause and effect between these two variables would be erroneous since several countries in the world have a high infant mortality rate but also have a fairly high life expectancy (Bolton, 2010).

DISPLAYING QUANTITATIVE DATA

Numbers are ubiquitous in history and the social sciences. They appear in histories ranging from nineteenth century U.S. domestic slave trade, to the Irish famine in the 1840s, to social science books and web sites about terrorism, influenza epidemics, and the death penalty. Numbers are extremely useful in expressing significant results, supporting thesis statements, or illustrating patterns, trends, and syndromes. They assist in establishing cause and effect and change over time. When displayed in some sort of graphical arrangement, they help the reader visualize patterns and relationships more quickly and easily.

As students cite and refer to numbers in their assignments, they also need to know how to display those numbers in the most meaningful manner. With the use of Microsoft Excel and many other excellent graphical display programs, this process can be both interesting and enjoyable, provided that students follow some best practices.

Many programs give students the opportunity to select from as many as seventy charts, tables, and maps. While this array is dazzling in its entirety, it also presents one with the paradox of choice. Students need to have a set of guidelines to assist them in making correct selections. In this section, a list of general and specific best practices and examples are included for several major types of graphical displays of nominal and ordinal data.

General Quantitative Display Best Practices

Allow the numbers to determine the type of display. Use a line graph for data over time, for example, to demonstrate the unemployment rate in three different countries from 1965 to 1975. Employ a bar graph for categorical data such as different governments' ownership of the postal service, gas, airlines, steel, and the automotive industries. For each type of graphical display, there are some simple guidelines that will ensure not only correct data visualization, but more importantly, mathematically correct depiction of the data.

Make the main findings easy to observe and comprehend. Use solids rather than patterns for line styles and fill. Furnish text alternatives for non-text elements such as charts and images. Use color appropriately to highlight different graph segments and when designing a map make color representative of water, forests, etc.

Aim for clarity with a graphic choice. The Y-axis scale should begin at zero. Have only one unit of measurement per graphic. Maintain the dimensional rule for graphics. If the data is two-dimensional, do not use a three-dimensional depiction because it will distort the data. Avoid the following: abbreviations, acronyms, labels that move from left to right, and legends unless they are on maps (UN Economic Commission for Europe, 2009a, 9).

Best Practices and Examples for Displaying Specific Types of Quantitative Data

While there is no code carved in stone for displaying quantitative data in tables, charts, and maps, there are a series of display type best practices that have been promulgated by several outstanding authors in the field of quantitative information displays. Their works contain useful advice and state-of-the-art visualizations of quantitative information.

Consulting the following texts is advised, especially for assisting students with strong quantitative data and computer graphic skills: Edward Tufte, *The Visual Display of Quantitative Information* (2001), *Envisioning Information* (1990), *Visual Explanations Images and Quantities, Evidence and Narration* (1997), and *Beautiful Evidence* (2006); Jacques Bertin, *Semiology of Graphics: Diagrams, Networks, and Maps* (1983); and William S. Cleveland, *The Elements of Graphing Data* (1985).

Table Display Best Practices

Tables are useful for displaying data that may be embedded in a text. They provide an instant snapshot of numerical information that usually takes the reader time to peruse and mentally categorize on a page or pages. Tables can be employed to make or reinforce a point within the text and usually support historical or social sciences analyses. Adhering to the following practices will help students in creating effective table designs and displays:

- The table title needs to present a clear and accurate description of the included data.
- Column headers are necessary to identify the data in each column of the table and to furnish specific metadata such as time period or country, etc.
- The first column of the table needs to identify the data cited in each row of the table.
- Any additional explanation of the data should be outside and at the bottom of the table in the form of footnotes.
- Attribution should occur at the bottom of the table and needs to include the name of the organization or source of the data.

- Tables need to feature only the most important aspect of the data that will be communicated in textual analysis.
- If referring to a span of time, maintain chronological order.
- Use a minimum of decimal places and round off numbers of the nearest decimal point (i.e., 104.5 rather than 104.52).
- Align the numbers on the decimal point to clarify their comparative values.
- Any missing data in a square should be noted as either "not applicable" or "not available" (UN Economic Commission for Europe, 2009b, 12–16).

Individuals Convicted of Public Corruption in Federal Prosecutions 2012

Federal Officials	369
State Officials	78
Local Officials	295
Private Citizens	318
Total	1060

Figure 2.1.   Example of a Good Table
Source: *Report to Congress on the Activities and Operations of the Public Integrity Section for 2012, 27.*

Tabular data may also be improved by using a new form of data display proposed by Tufte in 2006 called sparklines. They consist of "small, word-sized line charts that reveal trends over time." Their major advantage is displaying a significant quantity of information at a glance within words that explain their meaning (UN Economic Commission for Europe, 2009b, 44). The following example shows how the line chart was integrated into the table for an even quicker representation of the table data.

Reported Crimes and Arrests, New York City, 2001 - 10

	2001	2009	2010	10-year Trend	% change 2001-10	% change 2009-10
Index Crimes:	264,225	188,357	188,104		-29%	-0%
Violent Crimes:	68,737	46,357	48,489		-29%	+5%
Murder	649	471	536		-17%	+14%
Forcible Rape	1,533	832	1,036		-32%	+25%
Robbery	28,206	18,597	19,608		-30%	+5%
Agg. Assault	38,349	26,457	27,309		-29%	+3%
Property Crimes:	195,488	142,000	139,615		-29%	-2%
Burglary	31,564	18,780	17,926		-43%	-5%
Larceny	133,928	112,526	111,370		-17%	-1%
MV Theft	29,996	10,694	10,319		-66%	-4%
Adult Arrests:	298,654	341,003	343,308		+15%	+1%
Felony:	104,158	95,599	92,139		-12%	-4%
Drug	30,289	25,960	22,793		-25%	-12%
Violent	33,802	27,271	27,122		-20%	-1%
DWI	637	724	628		-1%	-13%
Other	39,430	41,644	41,596		+5%	-0%
Misdemeanor:	194,496	245,404	251,169		+29%	+2%
Drug	79,902	82,735	83,298		+4%	+1%
DWI	3,452	8,803	8,218		+138%	-7%
Property	50,451	77,516	81,810		+62%	+6%
Other	60,691	76,350	77,843		+28%	+2%
Adult arrests / Index crimes	1.1	1.8	1.8		+61%	+1%
Felony arrests / violent crimes	1.5	2.1	1.9		+25%	-8%

Figure 2.2. Example of a Good Sparkline Chart
Source: *New York State Division of Criminal Justice Services* in Klass, Gary M. *Just Plain Data Analysis*, 106, with permission.

Chart Display Best Practices

Although Microsoft Excel and other graphic display programs offer multiple types of charts for visualizing data, there are several basic charts and accompanying guidelines, along with their implied applications to all chart forms, with which students should be familiar. Charts are a more subjective form of visualizing data and thus amenable to wider interpretation. Unlike tables with their strict presentation parameters, charts can be designed in a variety of shapes, colors, dimensions, and scales.

It is their variability that presents the potential for misreporting on the part of the chart creator and misinterpretation on the part of the viewer. The benefits of using charts to display trends, projections, change over time, and cause and effect, however, far outweigh their limitations (Bolton, 2009, 1). Charts need to be employed when a table or textual explanation of a relationship would not be as apparent to the reader. Similar principles of table design apply to chart displays with some additions.

- Chart displays should eliminate the need for a written data summary for understanding the chart's message.
- Chart text should accurately define the representation of the data. Readers should easily grasp what any graphical elements equals or symbolizes.
- Comparisons drawn from numerical values such as how much or which event was larger or smaller provoke stimulating thoughts in the reader.
- Displaying numerical values that demonstrate change over time or the evolution of a variable highlights the accompanying text.
- Charts visually illustrate theses or the main objectives of the accompanying text.
- Chart data should be categorized around the most meaningful variable and never alphabetically.
- Let the data speak. Design, scale, and graphical icons should never intrude on the presented numerical information.
- Do not distort data to convey a message.
- Select the most relevant type of chart for the data. The data should always determine choice.
- When presenting more than one chart, be consistent with font, graphical elements, and type size (Klass, 2012, 83). (For demonstration purposes, this rule has been violated in this text to provide different cited examples).

Chart Elements

In his book, *Just Plain Data Analysis*, Klass (2012) states that most charts consist of "three basic components: the text, the axes, and the graphical elements." The text defines the chart's numbers by furnishing a meaningful chart title, axis titles, labels, and appropriate legends and notes. The axes, usually the Y axes and sometimes the X axes, represent the scale of the numbers displayed on the chart. Graphical elements display the magnitude of the chart's numbers and can be displayed in the form of bars, lines, pie slices, etc. (Klass, 2012, 82). Each of these elements has guidelines that if adhered to will produce appropriate and relevant charts.

- Titles should be descriptive and include the answers to what, where, and when without interpreting the data for the reader. It may also feature units such as the amount of U.S. dollars. The font is larger than other chart elements and is in bold. The data's source is included at the bottom of the chart using a smaller font and italics.

- Axes guidelines for the Y axis include minimizing the label space by including as few digits as possible and displaying the magnitude as part of the chart title. For X axis best practices, remember to horizontally align categories or dates. Make the text size smaller than the chart title, larger than the source title, and similar to Y axis labels.
- Graphical elements should be dictated by the data. Simple charts are better than complex ones. Pie charts are less comprehensible than bar/column charts, and stacked charts are less clear than a series of line/bar/column charts. Avoid unnecessary shading, color, borders around the chart, and gridlines (Bolton, 2009, 1–6).

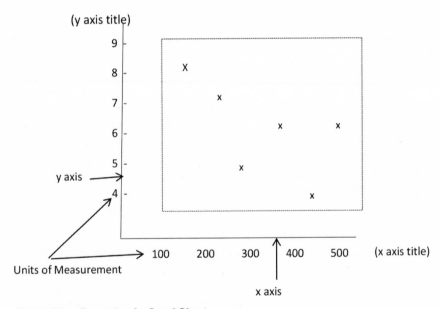

Figure 2.3. Example of a Good Chart

CHART TYPES

The dazzling array of charts presented in Microsoft Excel and other graphical display programs may bewilder many history and social science students just at the point when they are ready to introduce data to their projects in a new and interesting manner. It may easier for these students to understand that while there are numerous variations of charts, they are usually one of four fundamental types: pie; bar, time series, and scatterplot. Selecting the correct one is dependent upon the type of data they are working with and the data relationships that they wish to depict (Klass, 2012, 86).

Pie Charts

The pie chart is frequently employed by journalists in print and online newspapers because it is easy for the public to visualize. A pie chart shows the percentage distribution of one variable with only a small number of categories, usually not more than six. They are useful in enabling readers to comprehend the importance of one factor within the total (UN Economic Commission for Europe, 2009b, 21–22).

Of all the types of charts, Tufte and other experts at visualizing quantitative data, believe pie charts have the potential to distort data and misrepresent the scale of the data points. They need to be used sparingly by history and social science students. If students do employ them, adherence to the following best practices may alleviate some of their negatives when displaying data.

- Use pie charts judiciously. To overcome misrepresenting data point scales, consider labeling each pie segment with their actual values.
- Confirm that the data add up to a total of 100 percent.
- Two-dimensional pie charts present the best data depiction. Three-dimensional pie charts can easily introduce data distortion.
- Two pie charts should not be compared to each other.
- Sort data from smallest to largest values for easy comparison.
- Pie charts are preferable to doughnut, cylinder, cone, radar, and pyramid charts.
- Use pie charts to visualize the significance of one or more pie segments to the total (Klass, 2012, 87).

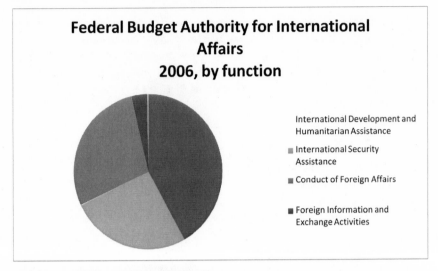

Federal Budget Authority for International Affairs
2006, by function

International Development and Humanitarian Assistance

■ International Security Assistance

■ Conduct of Foreign Affairs

■ Foreign Information and Exchange Activities

Figure 2.4.   Example of a Good Pie Chart
Source: *Historical Tables, Budget of the United States Government, Fiscal Year 2008,* 89.

Bar Charts and Histograms

Bar charts and histograms are used most often to present data characterized by discrete categories such as amounts, characteristics, times and frequency. They also help readers visualize a relationship quickly and easily. These types of charts can be either horizontally or vertically oriented. They lend themselves to comparing two or more values and are a visually appealing way to present quantitative data (Feinstein and Thomas, 2002, 36).

A histogram differs from a bar chart only in that the categories are ranges of values, with no overlaps and no gaps between values. The range is the same for all of the categories (Bolker and Mast, 2013). While Klass ranks them close to pie charts for efficiency in data presentation, because the data can be distorted, they do cause the reader to take notice perhaps more readily than textual explanations or a table display does. Bar charts and histograms also have a set of best practices for optimum display and reader edification.

- Resist the temptation to employ three-dimensional effects.
- Choose the most meaningful data element and sort from it.
- Any variable dealing with time should be in a left to right display.
- Reduce the number of colors and shadings.
- Insert legends either inside or below the plot area.
- Re-check the data input for potential distortion (Klass, 2012, 90).

Victims of Identify Theft 2012,
(by Type of Theft and Number of Victims)

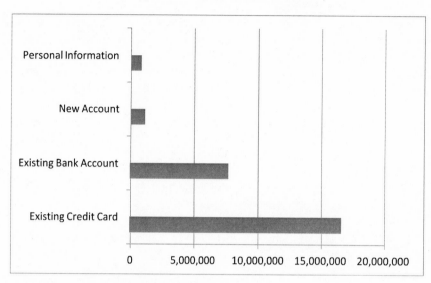

Figure 2.5.   Good Example of a Bar Chart
Source: *Bureau of Justice Statistics, Identity Theft, 2.*

Percentage of Voting Population That Was White (non-Hispanic)
in Last Five Presidential Elections

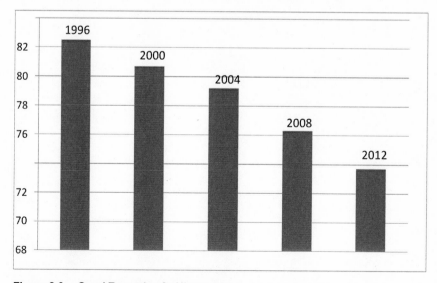

Figure 2.6.   Good Example of a Histogram
Source: *United States Census Bureau, Voting Population Measures, 5.*

Time Series Charts

Time series charts are used most frequently by historians and social scientists to display quantitative data about the movement of measures such as wages, prices, exports, crime, or agricultural yields over time. These graphs assist readers in visualizing and comprehending the chronology of the rise and fall of productivity, wages, jobs, or other variables that reveal seasonal fluctuations together with long-term trends. They are useful to help readers understand the relationship between two or more variables. Most time series charts involve a blending of descriptive and inferential statistics, but not at an extremely high mathematical level (Hudson, 2000, 9, 78). Time series charts also loan themselves to basic guidelines.

- Measure the variable of time on the horizontal or X axis and the movement variables on the vertical or Y axis.
- Label each line if more than one variable is depicted.
- Read the chart carefully to ensure that users can distinguish the lines for each variable.
- Show as much data rather than chart enhancements, icons, etc.
- Confirm that all variables to be compared are appropriately related.
- Be aware of potential errors of scale (Klass, 2012, 96; Statistics Canada, 2010).

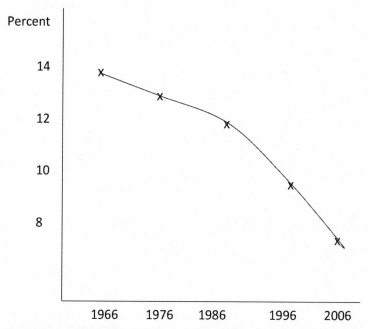

Figure 2.7.   Good Example of a Time Series Chart
Source: *Historical Tables, Budget of the United States Government, Fiscal Year 2008, National Debt*, **329.**

Scatterplot Charts

Scatterplots are sometimes referred to as line graphs because they require horizontal and vertical axes to plot data points. Their advantage over line graphs is to compare two variables and determine how much one variable might have been affected by the other. They are used most often to indicate correlation. If, for example, you wish to indicate the relationship between underweight children who are under five years old and their incidence of mortality in sub-Saharan African countries during the past ten years, this type of plot pointed chart is relevant. Scatterplots usually consider large amounts of data.

When plotted, data points that come close to making a straight line suggest that there is a strong relationship or correlation between the two variables. If the data points adhere to a straight line traveling out to high X- and Y-axis values, the variables suggest a positive correlation. If the line descends from a high value on the Y-axis to a high value on the X-axis, then the variables suggest a negative relationship. This type of chart is most useful for observational and experimental work. The only disadvantage may be when the data points are too numerous and dispersed for the reader to quickly grasp patterns and trends (Scatterplots, n.d.). Scatterplots also have some guidelines that assist in their construction.

- Ensure that there are two interval variables.
- Position the independent variable (the one possibly responsible for the movement of the other) or causal variable on the horizontal axis and the dependent variable on the vertical axis.
- Label both variables (plot lines) with the axis titles.
- Include both variables and the units of measurement in the chart title.
- Scale the axes to enlarge the plot area for showing the data points.
- Data labels are preferred to dots to eliminate viewer confusion (Klass, 2012, 101).

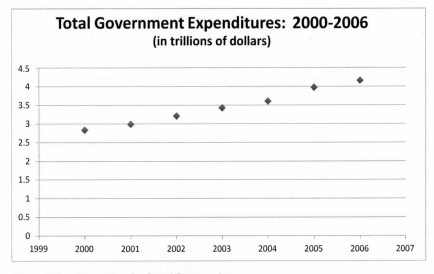

Figure 2.8.   Example of a Good Scatterplot
Source: *Historical Tables, Budget of the United States Government, Fiscal Year 2008, Total Government Expenditures*, 317.

VISUALIZING QUANTITATIVE DATA

History and social sciences students are no longer communicating their findings, assignments, term papers, and reports in traditional print formats. Quantitative data lends itself not only to table and chart displays but also to animation and video formats. All are important data visualizing techniques that students will need to be proficient with for the successful completion of assignments in the humanities as well as the physical sciences.

There are a number of outstanding web sites that provide free guidelines, sample charts, statistics tips, and step-by-step instructions for communicating quantitative data effectively. Several are commercial sites for well-known information visualization gurus such as Edward Tufte and Tushar Mehta. While these sites do not offer free downloads and directions, they do provide excellent illustrated introductions to some of these notable authors and their publications in the field of information display and communication.

Dr. Tushar Mehta (2013) has published several books about the use of Microsoft Excel software to visually display and communicate data. His commercial web site is filled with more than twenty free tutorials that can easily instruct students in creating custom charts ranging from horizontal line, step function, pie, three-dimensional surface, and stacked column charts. The "Tips" section of the site furnishes guidelines about how to analyze data organized in blocks and how to read the values of various points on a chart (http://www.tushar-mehta.com/). When students are ready to export their charted data, Mehta's site also features a section for preparing data-driven presentations with Microsoft PowerPoint software.

The "Data Visualization & Excel Charts" from Kelly O'Day (2008) contain visually explained dos and don'ts of graphically representing data. O'Day refers to various visual data display experts such as Edward Tufte and William S. Cleveland to confirm the dangers of creating a pie chart and features how-to links about the application of graphical interpretation skills and choosing the right chart for the type of available data (http://process-strends.com/TOC_data_visualization.htm).

J. Peltier's (2013) exhaustive A to Z index of Excel tutorials about almost any aspect of visual data display is a must for students to visit and use. Free instruction about where to click, illustrations, and sample charts are provided for every imaginable quantitative display including bar graphs, histograms, line charts, and scatterplots. Peltier, cited as a Microsoft "Most Valuable Professional," also includes a lesson for how to protect a chart or display once created (http://peltiertech.com/Excel/Charts/).

On par with Peltier's site is one called *The Spreadsheet Page* (2013). Students can search by categories ranging from formatting and formulas to charts and graphics. The screen shots are clear and concise, and the step-by-step directions are simple and executable. Both of these sites provide information for users only of Microsoft Excel software (http://spreadsheet-page.com/index.php/tips).

Another "Most Valuable Professional" site is titled *Charting Examples* designed by Andy Pope (2012). While not as robust as Peltier's site, this one contains an excellent tips link, instructions for how to create a variety of colorful charts, and an extensive series of links to other Excel visual data presentation professionals. Pope's site is worth visiting because the presented graphics are visually appealing to students who want to enhance their presentations with additional options (http://www.andypope.info/charts.htm).

StatLit.org (2013) is the only non-commercial site with information about visual data display. It features reviews about the latest statistical literacy books, web sites, and upcoming statistical literacy conferences. The best link to click on is under the subheading "Statistics Guides" and is titled "UNECE Making Data Meaningful Parts 1 and 2." Both sections of this document contain guidelines and illustrations of different types of graphics and examples of their relevancy and appropriateness to the questions posed.

These two sources are recommended for faculty rather than student use because they tend to be less tutorial and interactive in nature. The next link under "Statistics Guides" is labeled "UK Parliament Briefing Papers on Statistics for Policy Makers." Within this section are two papers with humanities-related examples titled "Guide to Statistical Tables" and "Guide to Statistical Charts," respectively. Both furnish excellent instructions for table and chart layout and formatting right down to the required punctuation and spacing (http://www.statlit.org/).

As part of the National Center for Education Statistics (2005), Create a Graph is an easy-to-use program that students can employ to create their own custom pie charts, line graphs, or scattergrams. Students can click on their desired graph, link to the data entry page, and choose up to fifteen data values. The site also allows them to select their graph size, color, and file type to import or print it.

ANIMATION AND VIDEO DATA DISPLAYS

Two data visualization techniques that are rapidly developing are animation and video. Their appeal to a generation that has been raised on YouTube cannot be overestimated. By integrating audio or textual description with charts and tables such as sparklines, these formats facilitate the telling of a story and make it easier for viewers to grasp the meaning behind the numbers.

The United Kingdom Office for National Statistics (n.d.) and Statistics Canada (2010) have produced dynamic population pyramids that feature interactivity with animation so that users viewers can click the "play" button to observe how the shape of the population pyramid changes over time. Users can also click on categories such as age groups to acquire detailed numbers and their proportion to the total population.

The co-founder of Gapminder, Hans Rosling, has employed animation to display data as a means of teaching statistics. Rosling has garnered not only an Internet following but his presentation at a 2006 TED conference has been downloaded thousands of times. His short "gapcast" video lectures on issues ranging from maternal deaths, globalization, and energy use have proved a popular medium for communicating data visualization techniques in a manner similar to Khan Academy's hundreds of math videos (UN Economic Commission for Europe, 2009b, 42).

One of the most exciting resources for faculty and students is the Statistics Online Computational Resource at the University of California, Los Angeles (2002; http://www.socr.ucla.edu/). It features a comprehensive set of free, Web-based tools for creating graphs, plots, and charts plus tools to assist in data analysis. Their interactive graphs provide excellent models for students to follow and develop.

DIG Stats (n.d.) sponsored by Central Virginia's Governor's School for Science and Technology (http://www.cvgs.k12.va.us:81/DIGSTATS/) is another site that provides valid data sets along with data visualization lessons so that students can acquire the skills to interpret the data and represent it graphically. Their instructions are clear and comprehensible and even include downloadable software such as Java's 3D Slicer applet with lessons on its applicability to enhanced data visualization.

REFERENCES

Bertin, J. (2011). *Semiology of graphics, diagrams, networks and maps*. Redlands, CA: ESRI Press.

Bolker, E., & Mast, M. (2013). *Common sense mathematics*. Retrieved from: http://www.cs.umb.edu/~eb/qrbook/qrbook.pdf

Bolton, P. (2009, January). Chart format guide. Retrieved from: http://www.parliament.uk/briefing-papers/SN05073

Bolton, P. (2010, July). Statistical literacy guide how to spot spin and inappropriate use of statistics. Retrieved from: http://www.parliament.uk/briefing-papers/sn04446.pdf

Bureau of Justice Statistics Identity Theft. (n.d.) Retrieved from: http://www.bjs.gov/index.cfm?ty=tp&tid=42

Cleveland, W.S. (1985). *The elements of graphing data*. Monterey, CA: Wadsworth Advanced Books and Software.

DIG Stats. (n.d.). Retrieved from: http://www.cvgs.k12.va.us:81/DIGSTATS/

Feinstein, C.H., & Thomas, M. (2002). *Making history count a primer in quantitative methods for historians*. New York: Cambridge University Press.

GapMinder. (2005, February 25). Retrieved from: http://www.gapminder.org/

Historical Tables, Budget of the United States Government, Fiscal Year 2008. (2008). Retrieved from: http://www.gpo.gov/fdsys/search/pagedetails.action?granuleId=&packageId=BUDGET-2008-TAB&fromBrowse=true

Historical Tables, Budget of the United States Government, Fiscal Year 2008, National Debt. (2008). Retrieved from: http://www.gpo.gov/fdsys/search/pagedetails.action?granuleId=&packageId=BUDGET-2008-TAB&fromBrowse=true

Hudson, P. (2000). *History by numbers an introduction to quantitative approaches*. New York: Oxford University Press.

Klass, G.M. (2012). *Just plain data analysis finding, presenting, and interpreting scientific data*. (2nd edition). New York: Rowman & Littlefield Publishers, Inc.

Mehta, T. (2013). Excel tutorials and tips. Retrieved from: http://www.tushar-mehta.com/excel/tips/

National Center for Education Statistics. (2005). Create a graph. Retrieved from: http://nces.ed.gov/nceskids/createagraph/

O'Day, K. (2008). Data visualization and Excel charts. Retrieved from: http://processtrends.com/TOC_data_visualization.htm

Peltier, J. (2013). Charting in Microsoft Excel. Retrieved from: http://peltiertech.com/Excel/Charts/

Pope, A. (2012). Charting examples. Retrieved from: http://www.andypope.info/charts.htm

Scatterplots. (n.d.). Retrieved from: http://mste.illinois.edu/courses/ci330ms/youtsey/scatterinfo.html

The Spreadsheet Page. (2013). Retrieved from: http://spreadsheetpage.com/index.php/tips

Statistics Online Computational Resource Center University of California, Los Angeles. (2002). Retrieved from: http://www.socr.ucla.edu/

Statistics Canada. (2014). Retrieved from http://www.statcan.gc.ca/start-debut-eng.html

StatLit.org. (2013). Retrieved from: http://www.statlit.org/

Tufte, E.R. (1990). *Envisioning information*. Cheshire, CT: Graphics Press.

Tufte, E.R. (1997). *Visual explanations: Images and quantities, evidence and narratives*. Cheshire, CT: Graphics Press.

Tufte, E.R. (2001). *Visual display of quantitative information*. (2nd ed.). Cheshire, CT: Graphics Press.

Tufte, E.R. (2006). *Beautiful evidence*. Cheshire, CT: Graphics Press.

UN Economic Commission for Europe. (2009a). Making Data Meaningful: Part 1. A guide to writing stories about numbers. Retrieved from: http://www.unece.org/fileadmin/DAM/stats/documents/writing/MDM_Part1_English.pdf

UN Economic Commission for Europe. (2009b). Making Data Meaningful Part 2. A Guide to Presenting Statistics. Retrieved from: http:// www.unece.org/stats/documents/writing/MDM_Part2_English.pdf

U.S. Census Bureau Voting Population Measures. (n.d.). Retrieved from: http://www.census.gov/hhes/www/socdemo/voting/index.html

U.S. Department of Justice. (n.d.). *Report to Congress on the Activities and Operations of the Public Integrity Section for 2012*. Retrieved from: http://www.justice.gov/criminal/pin/docs/2012-Annual-Report.pdf

United Kingdom Office for National Statistics. (n.d.). Retrieved from: http://www.ons.gov.uk/ons/index.html

Chapter Three

Social Sciences Sites

ACCIDENTAL DISCHARGES OF OIL

URL Address: http://oils.gpa.unep.org/facts/oilspills.htm#intelligence
   Site Summary: Some of the largest environmental disasters in the world
have occurred when liquid petroleum has escaped either from an oil well or a
ship containing it. The damage to human and marine life is difficult to measure since sea life and nearby land areas may be contaminated for years
afterwards. Students interested in environmental history will find this site,
sponsored by Global Marine Oil Pollution Gateway, a fascinating compendium of oil disaster related texts, charts, and statistics.
   Users can link to the *Oil Intelligence Report* that tracks oil spills from
1999 to the present, an *Incident News Oil Database* from the National
Oceanic and Atmospheric Administration that searches oil spills from 1984
to 2012, and tables of the world's sixty-three largest oil spills. The data are
robust at this gateway site and lend themselves to appropriate comparisons,
trend tracking, and future predictions.

Critical Thinking Lessons and Activities

1. Scroll to the heading "Mariner Group" and click on the link "Oil Spill
   History 1967-2002." Tabulate the data for oil spills, tanker accidents,
   and pipeline problems separately. Which areas of the world accounted
   for the most spilling of oil from 1967 to 2002? During this time
   period, which of the three oil spills were responsible for the most
   damage to the environment? Explain your choice of oil spills.
2. Scroll to the heading "Endgame Research Service" and click on the
   link "Major Oil Spills." Search the lists of spills and find the top five

countries that have experienced major spills from 1967 to 2010. Analyze the reasons why these countries have experienced more oil spills than other oil-importing and -exporting countries.

3. Scroll to the heading "Endgame Research Service" and click on the link "Major Oil Spills." By "2010 Louisiana," click on "US EPA response." At the "EPA Response to the BP Spill," click on the "Air, Water, and Sediment" data links. Analyze the data samples that show *exceeding EPA benchmarks.* Use this data to extrapolate the environmental impact that the British Petroleum oil spill may have on marine and human lives in the years to come.

4. Scroll to the heading "UNEP and OGP" and click on the link "Environmental Management in Oil and Gas Production." Scroll to Table 2 on pages seventeen to nineteen of the report. Read the data summaries for "human, socio-economic and cultural" impacts. Use the tabulated statements to argue that the human challenges associated with extracting and transporting oil far outweigh the benefits and that countries should pursue alternative energy sources more vigorously.

Related Internet Sites

National Commission on the British Petroleum Deepwater Horizon Oil Spill and Offshore Drilling
 http://www.oilspillcommission.gov/final-report
 Contains a detailed A to Z report with embedded data about the 2010 British Petroleum Deepwater Horizon oil spill that affected the U.S. Gulf Coast states.
 U.S. National Oceanic and Atmospheric Administration and Coast Guard Incident News Database
 http://www.incidentnews.gov/browse/incidents/by-date
 Searchable by incident name and/or date, this database is filled with quantitative information concerning oil spills worldwide from 1957 to 2012.

ANCESTRY: U.S. CENSUS BUREAU

URL Address: http://www.census.gov/population/ancestry/data/
 Site Summary: The United States has often been described as a nation of immigrants, and past and present U.S. Census data reinforce this statement. While many of the countries that produced our English ancestral heritage are no longer the main contributors to our cultural diversity, America continues to be a magnet for other nationalities seeking freedom and a better way of life. The ancestry section of the U.S. Census Bureau is replete with tabulated data from the 1990 and 2000 census years.

A separate link titled "Selected Historical Census Data" takes history students to ancestral information dating back to 1790, making this site ideal for comparisons among countries and regional groups such as Africans, Asians, and Latin Americans. Social science students can access the data for selected demographic trends.

Critical Thinking Questions and Activities

1. Under the "1990 Census," click on "Selected Characteristics by Ancestry Groups." Click on "Table 5 Population for Selected Ancestry Groups." Locate the top five ancestry groups with the highest percentage of United States entries between 1980 and 1990. Research the conditions or events in each of their indigenous countries that may have contributed to an ancestry group's desire to emigrate. Are there economic and social problems that these countries share? Write a term paper using these countries' problems as universal motives for high emigration rates.

2. Click on the "Census 2000" link and select "Historical Census Data 1790-1990." Click on "Table 2 Region of Birth of the Foreign-Born Population 1850 to 1930 and 1960 to 1990." The U.S. Civil War occurred between 1861 and 1865. Research the major historical events in Europe and Asia during this time period. How may these events have accounted for the significant increase in the foreign-born population during this turbulent time in America?

3. Under "1990 Census," click on "Selected Characteristics by Ancestry Group." Scroll to the bottom of the list and click on "Table 1 Educational Attainment for Selected Ancestry Groups." Find the top five ancestry groups who possess a bachelor's degree or higher. Return to the "Selected Characteristics by Ancestry Groups (CPH-L-149)" and click on the top five groups that you have identified. What correlations can you determine among these ancestry groups and the variables occupation, income, labor force status, and poverty rate?

4. Under "1990 Census," click on "Selected Characteristics by Ancestry Group." Scroll to the bottom of the list and click on "Table 4 Income and Poverty for Selected Ancestry Groups." Find the top five ancestry groups with the highest percentage of *persons in poverty*. Return to the "Selected Characteristics by Ancestry Groups (CPH-L-149)" and click on the top five you have identified. What variables appear to contribute to their poverty? If you were to develop a profile of an ancestry group that will more than likely experience significant challenges adapting and economically succeeding in the United States, what would it resemble? Be sure to include characteristics such as race, education, and the ability to speak English.

Related Internet Sites

The 1911 Census
http://www.1911census.co.uk/
Contains data from the 1911 census regarding population, etc., plus a special section about searching for ancestors and ancestral groups within Great Britain.

U.S. Federal Census Collection
http://search.ancestry.com/group/usfedcen/US_Federal_Census_Collection.aspx
In addition to providing links to previous census data, this site contains a highly specific search engine for researching one's ancestors.

ASSOCIATION OF RELIGION DATA ARCHIVES

URL Address: http://www.thearda.com/

Site Summary: Religion has played a role in every country's history. For some countries, such as Pakistan, the issue of religion was justification for its birth. Many social policy issues in different countries have religious implications that have created significant problems and challenges for their governments and people. The rights of women, for example, are limited in many countries based on religious doctrine and laws.

Although this searchable database focuses primarily upon American religions, it has constructed a robust archive of census data, maps, reports, and survey and poll results about the demographics and followers of various religions in other countries as well. Students can easily search and download data for the purposes of writing a full paper about some aspect of religion in history or use it to supplement a specific, developed thesis.

Critical Thinking Questions and Activities

1. Under "Quickstats," select "U.S. Congregations." Study two tables: "Politics by Region of the Country" and "Politics by Religious Tradition." Imagine that you are a political advisor to a presidential candidate. How would you advise her/him to address specific regions of the country about sensitive issues such as abortion rights, capital punishment, and gun control based upon the expressed survey data?

2. Under "Quickstats," select "U.S. Denominations." Click on "Judaism." Find a chronology of historical major events that affected Judaism from 1931 through 1990 and juxtapose it against the congregation membership data for a similar period. Be sure to click on the "Trends" link and study the two tables "Members and Congregation" and "Congregation and Clergy" for additional data. Discuss the factors that may

have been responsible for increases and/or decreases in membership and the number of clergy in Judaism relative to selected time periods.

3. By the link "Data Archive," select "Newest Additions." Scroll and click on the "Spiritual Life Study of Chinese Residents." Click on the "Codebook" link. Scroll to pages regarding individual questions and the response results concerning the role of religion in the life of the Chinese respondents.

   What historical events may account for the lack of interest in religion on the part of those surveyed? China is presently experiencing rapid economic and social changes, and some government officials have recommended educating the Chinese people about Confucian principles. Note the Chinese responses to questions about wealth inequality and other life questions. Based on these responses, what may it portend for the future role of religion in their society?

4. Often, political and religious rights are inextricably intertwined in certain countries, causing minority religion groups within these countries to suffer significant socio-economic hardships. Click on the "QuickLists" tab. Under "Compare Nations," select "Indexes." Click on the "Social Regulation of Religion (2005)," "Government Favortism of Religion (2005)," and "Government Regulation of Religion (2005)" links, respectively. Use the data to prepare tables showing the top ten nations where it would be disadvantageous to be a member of a minority religion. Discuss the economic, social, and political discrimination that members of minority religions might face regarding education, employment, and government participation opportunities.

Related Internet Sites

Adherents.com
http://www.adherents.com/
Furnishes sourced, census-based information about members of various religions according to the percentage in each country, the percentage of the total population, and the number of religious institutions established by that religion.

Hartford Institute for Religion Research: Religion Data Sources
http://hirr.hartsem.edu/sociology/research_datasets.html
Provides a webography of reliable and valid links to additional statistics about specific religions.

CHILDREN AND YOUTH IN HISTORY

URL Address: http://chnm.gmu.edu/cyh/

Site Summary: Children and adolescents are one of the most unrecorded groups in history because they lack the training and education to record the daily events and forces shaping their lives. Students searching for data about this population segment will find a primary source database consisting of 350 resources accessible initially by clicking on a broad region of the world. Many of the sources are textual, but there are a significant number that contain charts, percentages, and other quantitative information to generate a number of interesting questions and term paper topics.

The site also features sixty web site reviews of various online learning resources about the roles that children and youth have played in history, eleven teaching modules with sample questions and teaching activities, and twenty-five case studies with model strategies for employing primary sources in the classroom.

Critical Thinking Questions and Activities

1. In the search box, type "Love & Authority in Argentina [19cent.]." After clicking on the subsequent link, read the "Introduction" and click on "School Population in Buenos Aires, Argentina, Quantitative Evidence." Use the chart to show how the attendance rates changed between 1815 and 1831. Find additional data about school attendance during Argentina's Civil War. What do the attendance figures imply for government-sponsored public education? Discuss how can war affect children's lives in permanent ways.

   Find contemporary statistics for public education in Argentina. Is the government presently supporting free, public education for everyone? How might Argentina's past performance regarding education of their young people affect their economic development?

2. In the search box, type "Children during the Black Death." Click on the similarly titled link, read the "Introduction" and click on "Will-making among the general populace of Bologna during 1348 [graph]." Children were under a double threat from the bubonic plague. They not only faced death from it but, if they survived, they may have lost one or both parents. Incorporate the previously cited graph and some of the text documents into a paper discussing how children were the plague's most vulnerable citizens during this traumatic time in European history.

3. In the search box, type "Meiji Era School Attendance." Read the annotation that accompanies the tables. By 1872, Japan had drawn up a government plan of compulsory education for males and females

that was modeled on those of France and the United States. The table from the years 1873 to 1905 shows a pattern that is inconsistent with 100 percent compliance on the part of Japanese parents. What factors may account for the lack of enrollment and attendance during the indicated years?

4. In the search box, type "Age of Consent Laws." Read the annotation that accompanies the table. The age of consent is considered the age where an individual is capable of granting permission for sexual activity. Discuss how the increase in the age of consent from 1880 to 2007 in different countries reflects several factors including protection of women from prostitution, child marriage, teenage pregnancy, AIDS, and violation of women's rights.

Related Internet Sites

Children and Youth in America: A Documentary History
http://www.h-net.org/~child/Bremner/TOC.htm#Volume I
Provides hundreds of primary documents in the form of laws and other period essays regarding children's health, labor, education, families, etc., from 1600 to 1865.

Encyclopedia of Children and Childhood in History and Society
http://www.faqs.org/childhood/index.html
Supplies and A to Z full text dictionary of various terms, laws, trends, and issues about the history of children throughout the world.

CHILDREN'S DEFENSE FUND

URL Address: http://www.childrensdefense.org/

Site Summary: Much of the U.S. demographic data for an entire population focuses on employable, productive sections, usually adults between the ages of twenty and sixty. Children are often overlooked. Hence the need for this statistically laden advocacy site founded by Marian Wright Edelman in 1973 to address children's problems and issues regarding health, education, poverty, and living conditions. It also publicizes the latest research and best practices for trends concerning juvenile justice, income inequality, health and nutrition, family and community development, and social media concerns. Click on the "Research Library" tab to access all of the quantitative data.

Critical Thinking Questions and Activities

1. Under the tab "Research Library," click on "Archives." Click on the full text report "School Suspensions Are They Helping Children?"

which was published in 1975. Analyze the figures as viewed in "Table 1 15 Worst States in OCR Survey For All Students, Ranked by Percent Suspended and by Number Suspended." Research recent data and compare these state suspension rates with their most recent ones. Were there any changes for the better or worse? How do you account for these changes? Have these states changed their policies regarding suspension and are they publicly accessible?

2. Under the tab "Research Library," click on the link, "State Data on Children." Click on the reports "Portrait of Inequality 2012 Hispanic Children in America" and "Portrait of Black Children in America." Convert the percentage data under the headings "Poverty, Family Structure & Income," "Health," and "Education," respectively, to graphs that show the differences and commonalities between the two groups. What historical factors may be responsible for causing such inequality?

3. Under "Browse by Topic," select "State Data on Children." Click on the "United States" link. Use the percentage data to create a graphic profile of the status of children in the United States. Compare this data to the 2000 census. Based on these comparisons, create projections for the status of children in future years.

4. Follow the linkage directions in question 3. Select the percentages under the heading "Child Poverty in the United States." From the list of states presented, choose two each from the eastern, northern, southern, and western areas of the country. Select the percentages under the heading "Child Poverty." Create a choropleth map (a map using graded color values to represent relative data values) to show the variations that exist in child poverty among U.S. regions. Analyze the patterns revealed. What historical reasons do you propose that may account for these variations?

Related Internet Sites

Children's Rights
www.sos-us.org/
Furnishes news articles about issues involving the health and welfare of children in the United States and throughout the world.
International Bureau for Children's Rights
http://www.ibcr.org/eng/home.html
Contains information about child justice, the involvement of children in armed conflicts, and the sexual exploitation of children. Visit their newsroom archives for data and related articles.

CITY-DATA.COM

URL Address: http://www.city-data.com

Site Summary: Some urban researchers claim that cities preceded agricultural settlements. Economists surmise that they exist because of the need for easy trading of goods and services. Once erected, however, their rise and decline can serve as a barometer that historians employ in their research. The history of cities can be read in collected data such as employment, education, crime, housing, test scores, and pollution figures. Why some have continued to thrive during hard economic times and why some have descended into urban decay can be subject to intriguing historical analysis and opinion. This site is a treasure trove of statistics about thousands of U.S. cities. Students can use the information to assess and compare cities, track trends, analyze the effect of past events, and perhaps predict their future.

Critical Thinking Questions and Activities

1. Cleveland, Dayton, Toledo, and Youngstown, all cities in Ohio, have been identified as "rust belt cities" that are characterized by population and job losses. Under the "Cities" index, click on the link for "Ohio." From the following list of cities, select "Cleveland." Record the data regarding population and employment losses from 2000 to 2010 in graph form. Do the same for Dayton, Toledo, and Youngstown. Compare this data to the bar graph historical census from 1910 to 2010 for the entire state. How do you account for the demographic and employment changes that have taken place during this time period? What would you recommend city officials do to restore these cities to their former prosperity?

2. When an area of the country no longer seems promising to people, the first to leave are usually persons with higher education levels and employable skills. One of the first indications of a "brain drain" is a significant population loss among people of twenty to thirty years old. Data from the 2000 census indicates that the Midwest has been experiencing a "brain drain," particularly in Iowa and North Dakota.

   Select two towns or cities in North Dakota and Iowa that show a decline in population. Note the "educational attainment levels" of these towns or cities, *number of students attending school*, *average household income*, and *home ownership rates*. What would you recommend that these towns do to try and prevent their continual decline?

3. Crime rates may be an indication of a city's decline. Choose three known "rust belt cities" such as Gary, IN, Detroit, MI, or St. Louis, MO, and compare their crime rates versus the national average. Now

select three cities that have been designated as "thriving" such as Washington, DC, Austin, TX, and Seattle, WA. Perform a similar comparison of their crime rates. What factors may account for the differences or sometimes similarities in their rates?

4. The top ten "thriving" cities comprise Austin, TX, Seattle, WA, Boulder, CO, Salt Lake City, UT, Rochester, MN, Des Moines, IA, Burlington, VT, West Hartford, CT, and Topeka, KS. Choose four of these cities and analyze five common data elements that these cities share. If you were a manager of a major city, what recommendations would you make to city council members to ensure that your city continues to thrive economically?

Related Internet Sites

CityRating.com
http://www.cityrating.com
Furnishes extensive comparative data about U.S. cities.
Citytowninfo.com
http://www.citytowninfo.com
Includes information about the population, property values, education, climate, airports, etc., about thousands of U.S. cities and towns.

COST OF WAR CALCULATOR

URL Address: http://www.stwr.org/about/overview.html
   Site Summary: Richard Gabriel, the distinguished historian and author of *No More Heroes*, states that "nations customarily measure 'costs of war' in dollars, lost production, or the number of soldiers killed or wounded. Rarely do military establishments attempt to measure the costs of war in human suffering." *Share the World's Resources*, an advocacy site with consultative services at the Economic and Social Council of the United Nations, has created a cost of war calculator that enables one to actually note the cost of a specific armament and discover its monetary equivalent in, for example, the number of meals provided for starving people, clean water wells dug, etc. The site also features an issues section about global conflicts and militarization and poverty and inequality. Under the heading "Regions," users will find data-driven reports about different areas of the world and their humanitarian problems and relationship to war.

CRITICAL THINKING QUESTIONS AND ACTIVITIES

1. Use the drop-down menu to prepare a graphic depiction of the most expensive to least expensive weapons. Note the patterns in the resulting data. If you were a humanitarian, which weapons would you try to reduce in number? Explain your ideas and plans for arms reduction based on the data.
2. Ben Cohen, the co-owner of Ben and Jerry's Ice Cream, has testified before Congress in favor of military reduction. Distinguished military planners have concluded that our national security would be more than adequate if we reduced our defense spending by $40 million to $100 billion annually."[1] Scan the list of weapons expenditures and determine where you think such reductions could be effectuated.
3. Military actions have changed dramatically since the 1990s collapse of the Soviet Union. Prior U.S. military engagements (e.g., Korea and Vietnam conflicts) were much more expensive than recent conflicts in countries such as Iraq and Afghanistan. Imagine that you are the Secretary of Defense charged by the U.S. Congress with making significant budget cuts. Which weapons would you either reduce in number or perhaps eliminate in consideration of future conflicts?
4. The General Atomics MQ-1 Predator, also known as the "Predator drone," cost 4.3 million dollar per aircraft in 2010. Military strategists predict that this aircraft will significantly affect how future military conflicts are waged. How many predator drones could you purchase for the cost of a single B-2 Stealth Bomber?

Related Internet Sites

Costs of Major U.S. Wars
http://fpc.state.gov/documents/organization/108054.pdf
Prepared by the Congressional Research Service, this five-page report contains a table with the cost of all major U.S. wars and the percentage of the gross domestic product that each war cost in an individual peak year.
Costs of Wars
http://costsofwar.org/
This site, from the Watson Institute of International Studies at Brown University, contains data about the human, economic, and social-political aspects of the U.S. involvement in the most recent wars in Iraq and Afghanistan.

DEATH PENALTY INFORMATION CENTER

URL Address: http://www.deathpenaltyinfo.org/

Site Summary: Founded in 1990, this site is regarded by many jurists and criminal law scholars as "the single most comprehensive and authoritative source" on capital punishment. History and social sciences students will find reports and studies about various aspects of the death penalty and quantitative data from 1608 to 2012. The searchable execution database permits access and querying by year, age at execution, race of person executed, gender, state, race of victim, and method. A section on recent death penalty legislation and research about the efficacy of capital punishment is also included.

Critical Thinking Questions and Activities

1. Under the heading "Facts," click on "Executions by State, from 1608-1976." Find the top three states that had the most executions for this time period. Compare these states to the top three from 1976 to 2012. What do you think accounts for the differences in these states' rankings? One state has remained as one of the three from 1608 to 2012. Research and analyze the possible reasons.

2. Under the heading "Facts," click on "Murder Rates." Scroll through the data showing murder rates by states with no death penalty and those that have it. What factors might explain why the murder rate in states without the death penalty has remained consistently lower than the rates in states with the death penalty? All of the data has been adjusted for variations in state population sizes.

3. In the early nineteenth century, an abolitionist movement began to influence some states to abolish the death penalty. Under "Facts," click on "Executions in the U.S. 1608-2002: The Espy File." Examine the data from 1838 to 1860. Produce appropriate tables and bar graphs indicating whether this movement actually affected the number of executions during those years.

4. One of the major arguments against the death penalty is the significant financial cost to taxpayers. Under the heading "Issues," click on the link "Costs." Select "Financial Facts about the Death Penalty." Read the reports from each state detailing their capital punishment costs. Create a table displaying the incurred costs. Cite the data and write a legal brief in support of abolishing the death penalty for financial reasons.

Related Internet Sites

American Society of Criminology
   www.asc41.com/

Contains a broad collection of death penalty information, including government statistics, court decisions, and articles concerning the death penalty.

Death Penalty Worldwide
   http://www.deathpenaltyworldwide.org/index.cfm
   Provides a searchable database by country and geographic region of executions. The "Resources" section includes links to books, articles, and reports about the death penalty as well as some related web sites.

ECONOMAGIC

URL Address: http://www.economagic.com/

Site Summary: History and social sciences students can avail themselves of a wealth of retrospective and contemporary quantitative data concerning unemployment, personal income, housing values, interest rates, and household debt at this highly interactive site. One section provides the opportunity to create personalized charts from one hundred thousand economic time series in the database. Another section contains customizable reports that students can convert into Excel spreadsheets for personal analysis and manipulation. A third section, titled "Maps & Movies," features flash videos about employment data and yield curves. For students who are less confident with searching within such large quantities of data, the help section will be extremely useful.

Critical Thinking Questions and Activities

1. Under "Browse Data Collections," click on the link titled "Household Debt Service and Financial Obligations Ratios." The Household Debt Service Ratio is an estimate of the ratio of debt payments to disposable personal income. This debt reflects the amount of money that a person would need to pay for their mortgage and credit cards every month. This part of the database shows the Debt Service Ratio from 1980 to 2012. During these decades, there were two significant recessions: July 1981 to November 1982 and December 2007 to January 2009. In both recessions, the unemployment rate reached 10 percent. Note the years immediately following both of these periods. Does the Debt Service Ratio increase or decrease? What social and economic factors may explain these trends?

2. Under "Browse Data Collections," click on "House Sales." Scroll down to the heading "Number of Houses for Sale," and click on the link "US:NSA." A chart will appear labeled "US Houses for Sale: Thousands: NSA." Click on the chart. Now you have options to

change the chart results. Set the software to search 1963 to 2012 and have it show recessions. Keep all the other variables constant. Click on "Make chart." Research what types of recessions occurred during these time periods and the effect that they seem to have had on the ability of people to purchase homes.

What are the implications of people being unable to either purchase or sell their houses with respect to individuals who have lost their jobs and might be contemplating relocation to other geographical areas where employment opportunities may be better? How do decreasing home sales affect housing prices, and to what degree might this impact laid off workers contemplating second mortgages to cover their current expenditures?

3. Click on the "Reports" tab. Under "Annual Transformation Type," place a dot in "Average." Scroll to "Step 3: Select One Report Type," and place a dot in "State Unemployment Rate (SA)." Scroll down and click on "Create Report." Find the five states that have the highest unemployment rates for January 1990 and 2003, respectively. What industrial and/or economic factors contributed to the high unemployment rates in these states? Generate a similar report for the year 2012. Discuss whether the same patterns prevail.

4. Click on the "Reports" tab under "Annual Transformation Type," and select "Total." Under "Step 3," place a dot by the variable "Population by State." (This chart actually represents state annual personal income per capita.) Scroll down and click on the link "Create Report." Find the top five states with the highest annual income per person for 1990 and 2003. Research if they are still the highest in 2012. Why do you think these states have such a high per capita income compared to other states? If you were contemplating the opening of a new business, would you prefer to be in a high per capita income state or a low per capita state? Would it matter whether you were going to open a retail establishment, production, or service provider establishment?

Related Internet Sites

Bureau of Economic Analysis
  http://www.bea.gov/
Contains similar quantitative data along with the ability to download the information to Excel.

Lists of Randomized Sites for the Economagic Site
  http://www.economagic.com/help/hints.htm
Provides easy-to-understand examples of how to search the database.

ECONOMIC HISTORICAL DATA

URL Address: http://www.whitehouse.gov/fsbr/

Site Summary: Historical economic data is essential not only for understanding a nation's past but also for gauging its future. Although this web site's provenance is that of the current president of the United States, it contains a wealth of statistics and graphs concerning civil rights, education, poverty, healthcare, technology, fiscal responsibility, and more. Some of the data regarding the U.S. budget, for example, is recorded back to 1789. Students can use the statistics to support research papers on government and economic history.

Critical Thinking Questions and Activities

1. In the search box, type "historical tables." Click on the link "Historical Tables the White House." Select "Table 1.1 – Summary of Receipts, Outlays, and Surpluses or Deficits (-): 1789-2017." Budget receipts equal the income side of the budget. It is actually the revenue that the government receives in the form of taxes or other compulsory payments. Outlays are the expenditures that the government has to pay for items such as roads, schools, etc. Note the surplus/deficit column of figures beginning with the year 1850. Record and bar graph the sets of years showing when the U.S. Government experienced a budget deficit. Research what events were taking place during those time periods.

2. In the search box, type "Historical Tables the White House." Click on the link "Historical Tables the White House." Select "Table 3.1 Outlays by Superfunction and Function 1940-2017." Note the amount of money spent from 1953 to 1961 on national defense during President Dwight D. Eisenhower's term of office. President Eisenhower warned against the "rise of the military-industrial complex." What did he mean by this statement? Research how he tried to keep national defense costs down. Do you think that he succeeded during these years?

3. In the search box, type "Women in America." Click on the pdf report titled "Women in America." Scroll to the chapter on "Education" that begins on page fifteen. Design tables that present all of the gains. Social scientists are predicting that women will become the more educated and subsequently richer sex. Analyze the implications for this turnabout in terms of the traditional roles of men and women in our society.

4. In the search box, type "Your 2011 Federal Taxpayer Receipt." Assign each student in the class a dollar amount for "Social Security Tax," "Medicare Tax," and "Income Tax." Tell them to type these amounts into the search boxes and click on "Calculate Your Receipt."

Note how the percentage of their total income tax payment changes depending upon their assigned tax, social security, and Medicare amounts. Conduct a class discussion about how much of their tax dollars are being spent for defense as opposed to education. Ask each of them to act as members of congress and allocate a percentage of their tax dollars to the categories noted on the web page. Ask the imaginary members of congress to justify their allocations of their tax dollars.

Related Internet Sites

Income: It Ain't Where You Start, It's what You Got, and Where You End
http://www.econedlink.org/lessons/index.php?lid=65&type=student
This outstanding site contains data-driven lesson plans for examining income distribution and its relationship to poverty.

The Myth of Widespread American Poverty
http://www.heritage.org/research/reports/1998/09/the-myth-of-widespread-american-poverty
Although the 1998 data at this site is from the conservative think tank the Heritage Foundation, it is interesting to compare it to the present-day information for pre and post purposes.

HARRIS INTERACTIVE VAULT

URL Address: http://www.harrisinteractive.com/Insights/HarrisVault.aspx

Site Summary: Archived survey data is an important resource for studying past public opinion. Since the 1950s, survey data results have become an increasingly relied upon source of information for government officials, think tanks, legislators, and contending politicians. The data are often employed by government leaders to refashion the message that they are trying to deliver to the public. The "polls," as they are known, also serve as a barometer of a politician's chances for re-election or a political party's opportunity for passage of specific legislation.

Surveys can also have some negative aspects because people may be influenced to change their opinions. The Harris Vault offers a treasure trove of poll results from 1970 to the present day. Searchable by a broad number of subject areas, history and social studies students can discover what people actually thought about major issues, events, people, and problems during these time periods.

Critical Thinking Questions and Activities

1. Use the drop-down box under "All years" and choose "1970-1975." Click on the poll "Changing Views on the Role of Women (12/01/1975)." In November 1975, an attempt to pass an Equal Rights Amendment to the U.S. Constitution failed. Read the poll results and analyze the results regarding the feelings that respondents had about pro-women's rights groups not helping the cause of women or making a positive contribution to the cause. Based on the poll results, how might pro-women's rights organizations have to position themselves to ensure passage of the amendment?

2. In the keyword search box, type the words "Iranian hostages." Click on the link "Terms for Release of Hostages Most Met with Approval (02/02/1981)." In 1979, Islamist militants occupied the American embassy in Tehran, Iran, holding fifty-two Americans hostage until January 20, 1981. Read the poll results concerning this event. Describe how American government leaders may have been circumscribed from pursuing specific negotiations after learning of these poll results.

3. In the keyword search box, type the words "negotiated settlement Persian Gulf." Click on the link "Desire for Negotiated Settlement in Persian Gulf Prevails at Christmas (12/23/1990)." In August 1990, President Saddam Hussein ordered his troops to invade and occupy Kuwait. On November 29, 1990, the UN Security Council passed resolution 678 giving Iraq until January 15, 1991, to withdraw its troops or face a war to achieve their withdrawal.

   Throughout the twentieth and twenty-first centuries, other countries have accused the American people of militant tendencies. Analyze the poll results and discuss the significant number of respondents who favored a negotiated system or even appeasement as opposed to war. Compare these circumstances to Great Britain's plan of appeasement in World War II with Adolph Hitler. Should President George Bush have acceded to public opinion and continued negotiated settlement and appeasement policies longer? Could war with Iraq have been avoided? If so, how?

4. In the keyword search box, type the words "public tends." Click on the link "Public tends to blame the poor (5/3/2000)." America has been reluctant to adopt the socialist policies of many European countries that provide healthcare and other social programs to all of their citizens. Analyze the poll results about this topic. How are American beliefs about the poor reflected in our policies on healthcare and welfare? This poll was taken in 2000. Find a similar, more recent poll on this topic. Discuss how American attitudes have changed and the possible reasons why.

Related Internet Sites

Pew Research Center
http://pewresearch.org/
Under the topic "public opinion," students will find an archive of surveys and polls dating back to 2005. The site also contains a topic index with similar survey and report results within various social science headings.

Public Agenda for Citizens
http://www.publicagenda.org
Tracks public opinion particular on issues concerning education (kindergarten to college), energy, climate change, foreign policy, and the deficit. Click on the link "Research Studies" for archived surveys and reports.

HOMELAND DATA AND SECURITY STATISTICS

URL Address: http://www.dhs.gov/files/statistics/immigration.shtm

Site Summary: Formed in response to the September 11, 2001, terrorist attacks, the mission of the U.S. Department of Homeland Security is to protect the country from and react to terrorist attacks, manmade accidents, and natural disasters from within and outside the United States. To streamline hierarchical command structure and accelerate communication among other departments that may deal with terrorism, the U.S. Department of Homeland Security also integrated the Department of Immigration and Naturalization Service into its office.

Although overall immigration remained fairly stable after 9/11, the number of temporary visas and refugee admissions dramatically dropped. The Immigration and Naturalization Service part of U.S. Department of Homeland Security features a wealth of immigration, refugee, and asylee statistics that students can use to create profiles and portraits of refugee and asylum policies before and after the attacks.

Critical Thinking Questions and Activities

1. Scroll down to the heading "Yearbook" and select "Prior Yearbook and Data Tables." Scroll to the "1998 Statistical Yearbook" and click on the link "Refugees/Asylees." Click on "Table 27." Notice the increase pattern in the number of persons requesting asylum from 1973 to 1998. Research the major world events and U.S. refugee legislation that might account for so many people seeking asylum to the United States.

2. Scroll down to the heading "Yearbook" and select "Prior Yearbook and Data Tables." Scroll to the "2001 Statistical Yearbook" and click on the link "Refugees/Asylees." Click on "Table 21." Display the

Excel data results in a percentage pie chart for the years 1996 to 2000. Click on "Table 22." Display the top ten refugee/asylee countries data in a pie chart. Compare these tables with similar ones for the years 2002 to 2003. Discuss the reasons for the reduction in the number of refugees/asylees in the aftermath of 9/11.

3. Under "Immigration Statistics," scroll to "Nonimmigrant Admissions to the United States: 2011." Open the report and click on "Table 4." The United States has been experiencing an economic recession since 2007. What reasons may account for the continued significant nonimmigrant admissions to the United States on behalf of the top ten listed countries?

4. Under "Reports," click on "Publications" and then click on the link "Estimates of the Unauthorized Immigrant Population Residing in the United States: January 2011." Read the report. Refer to "Table 1," which shows the estimated unauthorized immigrant population from 1984 to 2011. Use these figures to project the estimated unauthorized immigrant population residing in the United States by 2050. Discuss the impact that this population will have in government services expenditures including education and healthcare.

Related Internet Sites

U.S. Department of Homeland Security Customs and Border Protection
http://www.cbp.gov/xp/cgov/about/
Click on the "Stats and Summaries" list for additional statistics regarding immigration problems and issues.

U.S. Department of State Trafficking in Persons Report 2009
http://www.state.gov/j/tip/rls/tiprpt/2009/
This report contains statistics about the extent of human trafficking in the United States since the U.S. Congress passed the Victims of Trafficking and Violence Protection Act in 2000.

LIBRARY OF CONGRESS COUNTRY STUDIES

URL Address: http://lcweb2.loc.gov/frd/cs/
Site Summary: Published by the Federal Research Division of the Library of Congress, this site contains online books about the economic, political, and social conditions of 101 countries. Although much of the data is in textual form, some data are presented in tables or graphs. Students need to carefully check copyright dates when comparing countries to ensure valid similarities or differences. The book publishing dates range from 1986 to 1998. In 2004, the Federal Research Division received funding to provide profile updates for selected countries. These can be found under the link

"Choose a Country Profile." It enables one to accurately compare a country's past data, displayed in the original online book, with its profile update.

Critical Thinking Questions and Activities

1. Afghanistan has seen little in the way of peace since being invaded by the Soviet Union in 1978, experiencing a civil war in the 1990s, and an occupation by UN-sponsored forces since 2001. Choose "Afghanistan" from the list of countries. Scroll to the section concerning health, birth rate, infant mortality, life expectancy, education, and literacy. Compare the information collected from the 1997 country study with the 2008 updated country profile. Display the information results in tabular form, and discuss how this country has fared over this thirty-year period.

2. The criteria for inclusion on the list of "Least Developed Countries" include issues regarding poverty, nutrition, health, adult literacy, and economic vulnerability. Click on the UN Least Developed Country list (http://www.unohrlls.org/en/ldc/962/) and choose one country from each continent. Return to the Country Studies and click on the "Search" link. In the keyword search box, type the word "economy." Refer to the list of countries and click on the three selected countries. Retrieve the data and record it. Use the data to compare each country's progress to present day. What do you believe accounts for their inability to be removed from the UN list?

3. Two countries that have made great strides on various economic and social markers that indicate a higher standard of living for their citizens are China and South Korea. Click and read through the original country study for each country and compare it to its updated profile. Select progress criteria such as education, adult literacy, poverty, gross domestic product, nutrition, health, and life expectancy. How have these two countries made such great strides during the past thirty years? What would you predict for their future based upon the figures that you have tabulated?

4. During the 1980s, Syria was thought to be one of the most stable countries in the Middle East. Then they experienced a serious drought, rise in oil prices, involvement with the civil war in Lebanon, and other financial constraints. Compare the original country study data with the updated profile for categories such as education, population density, and the number of young adult males versus the rest of the population. Imagine you are the U.S. Assistant Secretary of State. Use the data that you have gleaned to write a report warning your superior that Syria might become unstable during the next six years.

Related Internet Sites

BBC Country Profiles

http://news.bbc.co.uk/2/hi/country_profiles/default.stm

Furnishes accurate, current historical, political, and economic information about every country and territory in the world, accompanied by audio and video clips.

Countries of the World

http://www.factmonster.com/countries.html

Click on the individual country to retrieve updated information about the economy, political history, health, and other socio-economic conditions.

LITERACY RATES OF THE WORLD

URL Address: http://world.bymap.org/LiteracyRates.html

Site Summary: Literacy rates are computed as the percentage of a population that can write and read. They also serve as a barometer of a country's socio-economic status and an indication of its position on various rankings of countries on the rise or in decline. Literacy may seem like a given, but it is not in many parts of the world. In developing countries, one in four adults is considered illiterate. Wars, disease, and natural disasters can and do affect literacy rates in various countries. So can a country's leaders who realize the power that literacy can give people and work to reduce access to it through lack of education, restrictions to specific groups, and economic hurdles.

In the past, literacy rates have been measured using marriage licenses or certificates. If they were signed with a mark or an "X," that person was deemed to be illiterate. Measurement of literacy is now considered to be the ability to read and interpret simple sentences such as seen in a newspaper. For historians, literacy rates can serve as a means to research cause and effect and change over time in various countries.

Critical Thinking Questions and Activities

1. Botswana was once on the United Nations' "Least Developed Nations" list. Its 2003 estimated literacy rate is 81.2 percent. Other sites place this rate even higher for 2011. Research the reasons for Botswana's high literacy rate. Imagine that you are looking to outsource your business to an African country. Why might you choose Botswana based on their literacy rate alone?

2. Only seven countries and the Vatican City have 100 percent literacy rates. Compare their life expectancy, health, poverty, and employment rates with Guinea, Niger, Afghanistan, Chad, and Burkina Faso, where literacy rates are listed at 29.5 percent or below. Express the results in

a pie chart and discuss the implications for the future of the five lowest countries.

3. Iraq, Saudi Arabia, and the United Arab Emirates are oil-rich countries with literacy rates around 74 to 78 percent. By comparison, Brunei, Kuwait, and Azerbaijan are in the 92 to 99 percent range. What factors may account for the differences? What might the implications be for the oil-rich countries in the lower percentage when they run out of oil or if the world finds an alternative fuel source?

4. Somalia is considered by the United Nations to be a "failed state." Its 2001 estimated literacy rate is 37.8 percent. Discuss how this low literacy rate may have contributed to the civil war and subsequent decline of Somalia as a nation.

Related Internet Sites

Literacy Rate
http://www.sitesatlas.com/Thematic-Maps/Literacy-rate.html
Provides similar information about world literacy rates and includes a roll-over map showing percentages and world literacy rankings.

Measuring Literacy in Developing Countries from an International Perspective
http://www.stat.auckland.ac.nz/~iase/publications/3/TerrynI68.pdf
Written for the UN Educational, Scientific and Cultural Organization Institute for Statistics, this paper discusses the need for literacy statistics as a measurement and evaluation criterion for a country's socio-economic well-being.

NATIONMASTER.COM

URL Address: http://www.nationmaster.com/index.php

Site Summary: When students wish to research broad socio-economic categories such as education, government, terrorism, armed forces, or crime and compare data between or among countries, it is a challenge to collect all of the statistics and ensure that one is making apt comparisons and drawing the appropriate conclusions. NationMaster.com has compiled statistics for thirty social and history studies areas from valid and reliable government sources, and has developed a search engine that permits users to easily generate graphs and employ statistical indicators for research projects. Their sources range from the *CIA World Factbook*, United Nations, World Bank, and World Health Organizations, to the UN Educational, Scientific and Cultural Organization, UN Children's Fund, and the Organization for Economic Cooperation and Development.

The site features an encyclopedia, list of annotated statistical categories, A to Z country profiles, maps, a comparative search engine, and provocative lesson plans. World history students will find it useful when studying a theme such as democracy to research a country's past and see how far or little they have progressed to reaching their professed constitutional goals.

Critical Thinking Questions and Activities

1. India is one of the countries whose economy is starting to thrive because of globalization. Many Indians labor for wages that workers in more industrialized countries would consider unacceptable. These new jobs have helped to create an Indian middle class that historians believe is a healthy indicator of a thriving civilization. They also believe that for India to continue to develop economically, it needs a better education system. Use the "Compare any two countries" search engine and the education category to compare educational Indian statistics with those of three highly industrialized countries. How far and fast do you think that India will develop economically based on these comparisons?

2. Corruption continues to exist in every country. In many, however, it is endemic to society and it infects every transaction from obtaining a driver's license to permission for opening a new business. In many countries, it has crippled economies and dashed citizens' hopes for their future and that of their children. Government corruption can take the form of excessive red tape in the form of permits, inspections, and consultations to the payment of government officials to speed up the process.

   Use the "Search all" box and select "Government" as a category. Open the drop-down menu and research how the top five countries with the worst ratings compare for the following subcategories: "government time required to start a business," "start up procedures to register a business," "time required to build a warehouse," and "time required to enforce a contract." Use the results to discuss the implications for these countries to develop thriving and successful societies.

3. In the "Facts & Statistics" search box, choose "Terrorism" as a category and "collective political violence in 1990s with excessive targeting of civilians" as a subcategory. Examine the top five countries with the highest levels of political violence. Choose five countries with the lowest levels and assess their level of development. What effect has political violence toward their civilian populations had on their progress to date? Discuss the implications for the future.

4. Historians have researched the balance that a society needs between its productivity versus its national security. If, for example, a country

spends all of its resources protecting its borders, maintaining a huge army and manufacturing arms, and not enough producing commodities such as refrigerators and automobiles, it eventually produces a standard of living that may become intolerable to its citizens.

In the "Facts & Statistics" search box, choose "Military" as a category and "expenditures dollar figure (per $ GDP)," "expenditure % of central government expenditure," and "expenditures percent of GDP" as subcategories, respectively. Which five countries show the greatest imbalance? Analyze the forms of government that seem to characterize the nations that exhibit such security expenditure imbalances?

Related Internet Sites

CIA World Factbook
https://www.cia.gov/library/publications/the-world-factbook/
NationMaster used the statistics and data from this book to initially construct its database. It contains a wealth of data about the geography, economy, history, government, and communications of every country in the world.
Worldometers—Real Time World Statistics
http://www.worldometers.info/
Provides contemporary statistics about the world population, government and economics, society and media, the environment, food, water, energy, and health.

PEW GLOBAL ATTITUDES PROJECT

URL Address: http://www.pewglobal.org/
Site Summary: This division of the Pew Charitable Trust is chaired by former Secretary of State Madeleine Albright and former Ambassador to the United Nations John Danforth. Their focus is to record and summarize survey data about issues, attitudes, and trends affecting the United States and the world. The site features a publications section that incorporates the results of various public opinion surveys. Under "Global Indicators," a drop-down menu of topic questions links to a world map with responses displayed in bar graphs. Searchable by keyword and topic, the "Question Search" provides all of the survey questions posed since 2001. If students wish to use the data archive, they need familiarity with the Social Sciences Statistical Package (SPSS) and a login/account to download large files.

Critical Thinking Questions and Activities

1. Click on "Question Search" and select "Egypt" and "Tunisia." Select the topic "Economy" and the years spanning "2001-2011." Both countries have recently experienced what is known as the "Arab Spring," where they rid themselves of tyrannical rulers who had usurped much of each countries' wealth for themselves and their cronies. Look at the earlier years' responses to questions about the economy. As time passed, did Egyptians and Tunisians seem to be more optimistic or pessimistic about their economic future? How did their opinions serve as a forewarning of things to come?

2. Click on "Question Search" and select "Egypt," "Jordan," "Palestine," and "Israel." Select the topic "Israeli-Palestinian Conflict" and the years spanning "2009-2010." Note the responses to survey questions 1 and 2. What do these countries think of President Obama's handling of this continuing crisis?

3. Click on "Question Search" and type the word "economy" in the "Search for:" box. In the "Select topics" box, choose "China" from the drop-down menu and the years spanning "2001-2011." Note the Chinese people's responses to questions 1 to 4. How do they feel about the economic boom that they are beginning to experience? Summarize their responses and outline key recommendations for future U.S. relations with China regarding their economy.

4. Click on the "Global Indicators" heading. Find "Brazil" on the world map that appears and click on it. Under the "Change countries" drop-down menu are a series of questions that Brazilians answered concerning the "U.S. Image." Note the Brazilians' responses and incorporate them into a "diplomatic style" advisor memo that recommends how the United States should conduct itself vis -à-vis Brazil to ensure positive future relations.

Related Internet Sites

Pew Social and Demographic Trends Project
http://www.pewsocialtrends.org
Although this site is focused primarily on American social and demographic patterns, it does provide information on how they may affect the rest of the world.

Social and Economic Analysis—Key Areas of Focus
http://www.gallup.com/se/126851/key-areas-focus.aspx
Furnishes similar Pew survey and public opinion data about world economic and social trends with reports concerning their implications for the future.

ROPER CENTER PUBLIC OPINION ARCHIVES

URL Address: http://www.ropercenter.uconn.edu/

Site Summary: Established in 1947 to solicit public opinion concerning the events and social and economic trends of the day, this site contains a great deal of information that is free as well as sections that are fee-based. The fee-based part permits searching back to 1933, whereas the "Topics at a Glance" menu offers free access to historical survey data under rubrics such as economic issues and policies, education, elections, political parties and figures, government institutions, international affairs, and U.S. defense and foreign policy. Public opinion survey data is a useful accompaniment to reading documents and other primary sources that may be written from a government perspective. They serve to amplify the public's historical voice and opinion about how they actually believed and/or perceived the events of their times.

Critical Thinking Questions and Activities

1. Under the heading "Data Access," choose "Topics at a Glance." Scroll down to "International Affairs/Crises/Wars" and select "Latin America." Click on the link "Latin America Illegal Drug Trade and Latin America." The war against illegal drugs and drug-related violence has been an ongoing one with regard to Latin America. Read the three surveys concerning people's feelings about it. Research U.S. drug policies for the past ten years. Do you believe that American opinion about drugs and Latin America are justified by previous incidences of drug-related violence and transport?

2. Under the heading "Data Access," choose "Topics at a Glance." Scroll down to "International Affairs/Crises/Wars." Click on the link "European Union (EU)." The European Union was created for the purpose of becoming one of the world's most powerful and united trading blocs. Trace its history and development, and analyze the reasons for people's lower ranking of the European Union vis-á-vis the United States, China, and Japan.

3. Under the heading "Data Access," choose "Topics at a Glance." Scroll down to "International Affairs/Crises/Wars." Click on the link "Afghanistan." There are several polls involving this country where the United States has been at war for more than ten years. After summarizing the data from the various polls about Afghanistan, what course of action would you take if you were president of the United States? Would you accelerate the withdrawal of U.S. troops? Would you maintain some troops to try and maintain stability in Afghanistan?

How much would you count public opinion in your decision-making process?

4. Under the heading "Data Access," choose "Topics at a Glance." Scroll down to "Social Issues" and select "Human Rights." Click on the link "Rwanda." Note the results of the polls. In 1994, Rwanda experienced one of the worst genocides of the twentieth century when the Hutu-controlled government massacred more than five hundred thousand Tutsis, who were members of a rival Rwandan tribe.

Research the history of Rwanda. Was this the first time that Rwanda had experienced a genocide? Although the United Nations has rules concerning their involvement in any country where the government is committing atrocities against their own people, the case of Rwanda seems to have changed public opinion. Draft a set of rules citing public opinion and the evidence in the Rwandan genocide that argues for intervention by not only other neutral nations but also the United Nations if such an event occurs in any country again.

Related Internet Sites

Public Agenda for Citizens
http://www.publicagenda.org/
Provides non-partisan public opinion data about a variety of issues concerning the United States.

World Association for Public Opinion Research
http://wapor.unl.edu/
Pollsters and researchers try to furnish non-biased opinion research data about global issues.

STATISTICAL ABSTRACT OF THE UNITED STATES

URL Address: www.census.gov/compendia/statab/hist_stats.html

Site Summary: The U.S. Census Bureau has been compiling yearly statistics about the social and economic conditions of the country since 1878. Divided into thirty browsable sections, the abstract contains 1,300 tables of statistics concerning over two hundred topics such as crime, income, poverty, energy, science and technology, and elections. Much of the information spans more than twenty years and lends itself to historical analysis. The majority of the tables are in PDF or Excel formats for easy manipulation into graphs and other display media.

Critical Thinking Questions and Activities

1. Under the "Browse Sections:" heading, scroll to the "Income, Expenditure, Poverty, & Wealth" link. Select the subsection "Personal Income," and click on the link "Personal Income Per Capita in Current (2005) Dollars by State 1980-2010." One of the most concrete measures of a country's economic state is termed per capita income. Economists calculate this figure by dividing the annual national income by the total population of a country. Compare the U.S. national per capita income with that of Alabama, Mississippi, and Georgia. Why are their per capita incomes lower than the national average per capita income? Find statistics that go back farther and discuss their historical implications.

2. Under the "Browse Sections:" heading, scroll to the "Income, Expenditure, Poverty, & Wealth" link. Select the subsection "Personal Income," and click on the link "Individuals and Families below Poverty Level – Number and Rate by State: 2000 and 2009." Use the table to find the top five states with the most people living below the poverty level in 2000 and 2009, respectively. Have the top five states changed during this period? Display the information in a bar graph and discuss specific causative factors such as unemployment and increased immigration.

3. Under the "Browse Sections:" heading, scroll to "Education" and choose "Education: Elementary and Secondary Education: Technology, Courses, and SAT Scores 1970-2010." Click on the link "267 SAT Scores and Characteristics of College-Bound Seniors." Examine the test scores for all the years in the area of "Critical Reading and Math." What factors may account for the continued decline in the "Critical Reading" scores? Discuss the implications of this trend for the United States in a competitive, global economy. Assume that you are the U.S. Secretary of Education. What specific recommendations would you propose that American schools do to remedy the situation?

4. Under the "Browse Sections:" heading, scroll to "Labor Force, Employment, & Earnings," and select "Table 635 Labor Force, Employment & Earnings: Job Gains and Losses." From 2000 to 2008, the United States has experienced a form of creative destruction with the loss of many manufacturing jobs to countries that could do the work for less pay. Although there has been some job creation, it has not been in the same areas that have historically seen significant growth.

    Analyze "Table 635" for the trends in job loss and gains. What sectors of the job market have seen the most loss? Look at "Table 636" and examine the five states that have experienced the most job losses. What sectors of the economy were they? How would you go about restoring jobs to these states?

Related Internet Sites

American FactFinder
http://factfinder2.census.gov/faces/nav/jsf/pages/index.xhtml
Provides a search engine for finding various economic and social information about the United States.

The 2012 Statistical Abstract of the United States: Earlier Editions
http://www.census.gov/compendia/statab/past_years.html
Earlier editions of the abstract provide history students with the means for making additional comparisons and tracing patterns for previous years. This site is helpful for answering question 1.

SUBSTANCE ABUSE AND MENTAL HEALTH ADMINISTRATION

URL Address: http://www.samhsa.gov/

Site Summary: Drug abuse, suicide, and mental health disorders are often the result of socio-economic factors that are impacting a nation. Poverty, unemployment, homelessness, discrimination, and previous military service place people at increased risk for suicide, drug abuse, and other mental health problems. Cultural historians analyze data about the frequency, rate, and treatment of substance abuse and mental illness to gauge a nation's ability to create a society where people have a sense of optimism and hope in the future. This government agency site has a "Data, Outcomes, and Quality" section that contains statistics and graphs about drug abuse, behavioral treatment, and suicide rates from 1989 to 2012. It enables students to study the increases or decreases in substance abuse and mental health problems in light of the major political, military, and cultural events of the day.

Critical Thinking Questions and Activities

1. In the site's search box, type the words "Suicide Veterans Military." Click on the link "Serious Psychological Distress and Substance Use Disorder." Use the data presented in Figures 1 to 4 to discuss the reasons why so many veterans of military wars in Iraq and Afghanistan are suffering from these disorders. How do you account for the significant differences between women and men with regard to substance use disorder? Why do those with incomes below a certain amount seem to suffer from these disorders at a higher rate than their peers?

2. Visit this address at Samhsa's web site: http://www.samhsa.gov/data/
   NSDUH.aspx. Under the heading "What's New," click on the link
   "Results from the 2010 National Survey on Drug Abuse" and "Health:
   Mental Health Findings and Detailed Tables." Scroll to and then click
   on the link "Major Depressive Episode and Substance Use Disorder
   among Youth." Use the data displayed in the various figures about
   depression and substance abuse among youth and discuss the implications for treatment plans in a time of the Great Recession.
3. Return to the report titled "Results from the 2010 National Survey on
   Drug Use and Health: Mental Health Findings." Scroll to "4. Co-
   Occurring Mental Health and Substance Use Disorder among Adults,
   by Demographic and Socio-Economic Characteristics." Use the data
   figures to create a ranked factor profile of Americans who are most
   prone to mental illness and substance abuse. Discuss which factors
   seem to create the environment for mental illness and drug abuse to
   flourish within this demographic segment of the population.
4. Return to the "What's New" section of the site at http://
   www.samhsa.gov/data/NSDUH.aspx. Scroll to "2001" and click on
   "Summary of Findings from the 2000 National Household Survey on
   Drug Abuse." Click on "TOC" and open the link titled "2. Illicit Drug
   Use." Read the report and study the figures to determine which illicit
   drugs are used most frequently. Given the cost of imprisoning people
   for using these drugs, are there any that you might legalize? Use the
   data to support your argument for or against the legalization of any or
   all of the named illicit drugs.

Related Internet Sites

National Institutes of Health
   http://health.nih.gov/
   Provides additional information and data about the use and abuse of drugs
and incidences of mental illness.
National Strategy for Suicide Prevention
   http://www.samhsa.gov/prevention/suicide.aspx
   This division of the U.S. Substance Abuse and Mental Health Administration contains useful data about the suicide, the primary cause of death
among adolescents and adults under the age of thirty-five.

TERRORISM

URL Address: http://smapp.rand.org/rwtid/search_form.php
   Site Summary: The world experiences terrorism in many forms including religious, political, ideological, and even state-sponsored. It is a cruel

form of violence because the perpetrators choose those who are considered non-combatants as their victims. Terrorist groups have the potential for inflicting much more damage now because of their access to sophisticated and remote-based technologies. After 9/11, the United States became much more vigilant and proactive regarding terrorist groups.

This site, founded by Rand Corporation, has been maintaining a database of domestic and international terrorism incidents from 1968 to 2009. The database contains more than thirty-six thousand incidents of terrorism coded and summarized in complete detail and searchable by date, numbers of injuries, tactics, weapon, country, perpetrator, and target. Students can elect to display the results as a list, pie chart, or as an aggregated chronological graph. The site also contains hundreds of reports that analyze terrorism patterns within groups and countries.

Critical Thinking Questions and Activities

1. In "RWCDATI"I search boxes, scroll to the one labeled "Perpetrator." Select "Provisional Irish Republican Army (PIRA)" and click on "Submit." After the list of incidents appear, click on "Data export file." The results will convert to a manipulatable Excel file. Use the data results as a terrorism timeline. As the bombings escalated, was there any change in the British government's response to demands that Northern Ireland be removed from the United Kingdom? What conclusions can you draw regarding the effectiveness of their campaign?

2. In the "Perpetrator" search box, select "Shining Path (SL)," which also stands for Sendero Luminoso, the name of a Peruvian terrorist organization. Click on "Submit." After the data loads, click on "Data Export." The Shining Path was founded by a Maoist professor named Abimael Guzman. He was captured in 1992. Graph the number of terrorist incidents before and after Guzman's capture. Note the results. What conclusions can you draw about the power of one person to incite violence?

3. In the "Perpetrator" search box, select "Baader-Meinhof Group." Click on "Submit." After the incident data loads, click on "Data Export." Repeat the procedure for the "Red Army Faction" and the "Revolutionary Cells," respectively. From 1970 to 1998, West Germany and then a united Germany suffered from terrorism by several post–World War II left-wing military groups. Analyze the data and compare each group. Which one caused the most fatalities? If you were in charge of security forces in Germany, which one would you have feared the most? Why?

4. In the "Perpetrator" box, select "Revolutionary Armed Forces of Columbia (FARC)." Click on "Submit." After the incident data loads,

click on "Data Export." Choose incidents with fatalities numbering ten or more people. This terrorist organization has been functioning in Columbia for forty-eight years. Analyze why these types of targets may enable the Revolutionary Armed Forces of Columbia to be tolerated by so many Columbians.

Related Internet Sites

Database of Terrorist Attacks
http://www.people.haverford.edu/bmendels/terror_attacks
Provides a list of annotated links to various terrorist tracking sites.
National Security Institute
http://nsi.org
Contains information related to many terrorism topics, including data on recent attacks.

UN HIGH COMMISSION FOR REFUGEES

URL Address: http://www.unhcr.ch/
Site Summary: The United Nations officially terms people who have been granted temporary or permanent protection on humanitarian grounds "refugees or internally displaced persons." The agency took responsibility for monitoring their movements and meeting their basic needs and attempting to repatriate them when the League of Nations ended in 1946. The main impetus was the refugee crisis that occurred after World War II when hundreds of nations were awash in stateless and homeless people.

Since that time, the UN High Commission for Refugees has maintained an archive of records of all events involving refugees and internally displaced persons. Under the "RESOURCE" drop-down menu, their web site provides access to reports and publications filled with quantitative data spanning 1999 to 2013, maps, and a statistical and operational data section. The site also features a "Browse by Country" drop-down menu that permits comparisons of the movement of refugees and internally displaced persons between and among other countries.

Critical Thinking Questions and Activities

1. In the "Browse by Country" search box, choose "Sudan" and "Afghanistan." Note the number of displaced persons for each country. Compare this data to that of France and Switzerland. Research the events that are causing the high numbers of internally displaced persons in Afghanistan and Sudan. Analyze the effects that these numbers

of displaced persons are having on their developmental progress. Analyze the numbers of internally displaced persons in Switzerland and France. How do these low numbers affect their developmental progress?

2. Under the heading "Resources," select "Statistics & Operational Data" and click on "Syria Regional Refugee Response." Syria is currently involved in a civil war. The majority of Syrians are fleeing to Turkey, Lebanon, Jordan, and Iraq. Research each country's ability to care for these refugees. Some of these countries are experiencing political instability themselves. Discuss what the political effects large populations of Syrians living in refugee camps may have on each country's respective government.

3. Asylum cannot be granted by the United Nations. Each country has its own rules and conditions that applicants must meet before they will grant asylum. Under "RESOURCES," click on "Statistics & Operational Data" and choose "UNHCR Statistical Yearbooks." Select "Statistical Yearbook 2010" and click on "Chapter 4 Asylum and Refugee Status Determination." Read the chart in the chapter titled "Main countries of origin of new asylum-seekers 2010." Note which countries had between 75,000 and 150,000 persons seeking asylum. Use this list and compare the year 2010 with selected previous Statistical Yearbooks. If you were the high commissioner for the United Nations, where would you target your resources to help asylum seekers? What resources would you try and make available to them?

4. Under "Statistics & Operational Data," select "Millennium Development Goals" and click on the "Millennium Development Goals (MDGS")" link. Select "End poverty and Hunger." Examine the data concerning "targets 1A-1C." What does the UN High Commission for Refugees have to do to reach its millennium goals? Describe some of the problems thwarting them?

Related Internet Sites

Bureau of Population, Refugees and Migration
  http://www.state.gov/j/prm/
This U.S. government agency site contains statistics and other data about refugees, asylum seekers, and more.

Migration Information Source—Global Data Center
  http://www.migrationinformation.org/GlobalData/
The migration data at this site allows students to track, analyze, chart, map, and track trends in human migration from the 1950s to the present day.

WOMENWATCH

URL Address: http://www.un.org/womenwatch/

Site Summary: Women comprise approximately 51 percent of the world's population. In many parts of the globe, however, their status is significantly inferior to that of men, particularly in developing countries. The United Nations has highlighted the need for special attention to the needs and rights of women through various programs, conferences, and collections of data that document the disparity that exists between men and women in many countries of the world.

At the WomenWatch site, history and social studies students will discover data-derived reports, charts, and goals that give them the information to trace whether progress has occurred since the UN-sponsored conference on women in Beijing in 1995. This bellwether conference issued a call to action on the part of member countries to develop national action plans to improve the status of women in their respective countries.

Critical Thinking Questions and Activities

1. Click on "Status and Indicators." Scroll down to the heading "The World's Women," and click on "The World's Women: Trends and Statistics 2010." Scroll to "Statistical Annex" and click on the link "Chapter 5 Power and Decision-making." Find the top five countries where women have power and decision-making capabilities, and compare them to the top five countries where women have little or no power. Create a bar graph for each category that shows where each country ranks. Analyze the characteristics of each of these countries in terms of their form of government and structure that might be reasons why some have empowered women and others have not.

2. Click on "Status and Indicators." Scroll down to the heading "The World's Women," and click on "The World's Women: Trends and Statistics 2010." Scroll to "Statistical Annex" and click on the link "Chapter 6 Violence against Women." Find which region of the world has the highest "prevalence of violence against women." Use the statistics from the top three countries where violence is most prevalent against women to create a public awareness campaign to help stop it. Create three posters for each country that take into account that country's major religion, customs, form of government, and laws.

3. Click on "Status and Indicators." Scroll down to the heading "The World's Women," and click on "The World's Women: Trends and Statistics 2010." Scroll to "Statistical Annex" and click on "Chapter 2 Health." Maternal mortality is influenced by a number of factors including the number of pregnancies, the lack of contraception, poor

nutrition, and deliveries without the assistance of skilled medical personnel. Scroll through Table 2.A and identify each country in Africa, Asia, Latin America, and the Caribbean that has the "highest mortality per 100,000 live births." Research what is needed to lessen maternal mortality and prepare a "United Nations" aid grant for each country that you believe would lessen the maternal mortality.

4. Click on "Status and Indicators." Scroll down to the heading "The World's Women," and click on the link "The World's Women: Trends and Statistics 2010." Scroll to "Statistical Annex." Click on "Chapter 8 Poverty." Having no access to cash or having no say in how your own earned income is spent is a recipe for guaranteed poverty as a woman. In many countries, women are poverty-stricken because of these two conditions. Identify the top five countries that keep women in poverty by these two means. Use the statistics to initiate a plan for these countries that includes their participation in small loans projects such as those at Kiva.org, etc. Draft an exemplary law for these countries that guarantees women economic freedom within the family household.

Related Internet Sites

Gender
http://www.fao.org/gender/en/
The Food and Agriculture Organization of the United Nations maintains an informative section on women that focuses on equality of gender with regard to employment in agriculture.

World Bank Gender Equality and Statistics
http://datatopics.worldbank.org/gender/
Statistics at this gender data portal are organized under headings including education, health and related services, public life and decision-making, human rights of women and girl children, and demographic indicators.

WORLD BANK DATA

URL Address: http://data.worldbank.org/
Site Summary: The World Bank is much more than a traditional loan institution. It is an internationally respected source for economic and technical expertise to developing countries around the globe. Consisting of 188 member countries, the World Bank's focus is on fighting poverty, assisting countries in conflict, and providing education and training to nations in need. This web site contains a treasure trove of comparative data about agriculture, climate change, health, education, energy, environment, and gender issues. Analyses of the cumulated data can serve as historical and social sciences

indicators of the world's progress in alleviating suffering and improving the lives of millions of people.

Critical Thinking Questions and Activities

1. Under the "By Topic" tab, click on the "Poverty" link. Study the interactive map titled "Poverty headcount ration at $1.25 a day (PPP) (% of population)." Use the cursor to roll over the sub-Saharan African countries. Record which ones have the highest percentage of poverty. Research the agricultural, climate, employment, and political factors that may account for their acute poverty.

2. Under the "By Topic" tab, click on the "Poverty" link. Click on the link titled "Poverty Gap at $2 a day (PPP) (%)." Historians and social scientists have written about alleviating poverty with skepticism in many developing countries. Click on each set of years (1980 to 2012) and create a bar graph for Brazil's poverty rate. What pattern do you observe over time? How has Brazil been able to lower its poverty rate? Be sure to include information about agrarian reform, anti-corruption campaigns, and the use of natural resources.

3. Under the "By Topic" tab, click on the "Education" link. Social scientists know that there is a positive correlation between education and poverty. In many developing countries, however, women do not progress to the secondary educational level. Click on "Progression to Secondary School male (%)" and the corresponding link for female. Select three countries where the females do not progress to secondary school and compare these countries' corresponding poverty rates. Employ the findings to show how essential it is for a country to have both genders educated at the secondary level.

4. Under the "By Topic" tab, select "Health." Click on two links: "Prevalence of HIV female (% ages 15-24)" and the corresponding link for males. AIDS in many developing countries afflicts females in greater numbers than it does males. Select the five countries with the highest female HIV prevalence and compare their rates to the male prevalence. Create a pie chart showing the disparity for each country. Imagine that you have been appointed secretary of the department of health and human services for one of these countries. How would you employ this evidence to develop a medical and education AIDS prevention plan that especially targets females?

Related Internet Sites

Human Development Reports
   http://hdr.undp.org/en/reports/global/hdr2011/

Published by the United Nations, this site furnishes similar quantitative data about the topics presented in the World Bank site.

International Monetary Fund
http://www.imf.org/external/data.htm
Although much of the data and statistics are financial, this site contains useful data about the economic outlook for developing countries.

YOUTH INDICATORS

URL Address: http://nces.ed.gov/programs/youthindicators/
Site Summary: Presented in tabulated form, this database of statistics about Americans between the ages of fourteen and twenty-four is a robust compendium of historical and social studies information about the demographic distribution of young people, their family constellations, employment status, after school engagements, and health and welfare. The data are collected by the National Center for Education Statistics and are used to analyze and plan future government programs and support for young people. History and social sciences students will discover that current and past *Youth Indicators* reports furnish them with historical data as far back as 1960, which gives them the opportunity to trace the impact of various economic and historical events over time.

Critical Thinking Questions and Activities

1. Click on "Chapter 1 Demographics." Under "Indicator 1," notice that the data reveals that "the proportion of youth and young adults ages 14 to 24 declined from 20 percent of the U.S. population in 1980 to 15 percent in 2010." Incorporate "Table 1" data and "Figure 1" data into a PowerPoint or Prezi presentation that includes the implications of this finding for future health care and social security programs that the younger generation is expected to support through their employment.

2. Click on "Chapter 1 Demographics." Under "Indicator 4," observe that the data reveal that "a greater percentage of young adults ages 20 to 24 were living with their parents in 2010 (42 percent) than in 1980 (38 percent)." In addition, "more young adults lived with relatives who were not their spouse or parent or lived with related and unrelated subfamilies in 2010 than in 1980 (12 vs. 6 percent)." Discuss the economic and social conditions that may have contributed to this demographic change. Use the percentage of change and project the percentages until 2015. What percentage of young adults aged twenty to twenty-four may be expected to be living under these same arrangements then?

3. Click on "*Chapter 2 School-Related Characteristics.*" Under "*Indicator 8*," note that the data shows "for older youth, the current generation is enrolled in school at consistently higher rates than previous ones were." Use "Table 8" and "Figure 8" data to support this statement. Discuss the reasons why so many young people are still enrolled in school rather than in the labor force.

4. Click on "Chapter 3 Employment-Related Characteristics." Under "Indicator 31 Poverty," note that the data show that the "poverty rate increased from 14 to 20 percent between 2000 and 2009." This increase occurred for "both male (from 12 to 17 percent) and female (from 16 to 22 percent) 15- to 24-year-olds between 2000 and 2009." Find a history timeline of events that happened between these years. Impose the timeline in the form of a mash-up to show which events may have helped cause the increase in the poverty rate for young adults during these years.

Related Internet Sites

World Youth Report
  http://social.un.org/index/WorldYouthReport/2012.aspx
  While the data is not tabulated as it is in *Youth Indicators* reports, this site contains chapters describing the percentages of young people: living in poverty, employed, jobless, and educated throughout the world. It also provides a convenient link to previous reports dating to 2003.
Youth Indicators 1996
  http://nces.ed.gov/pubs98/yi/
  This *Youth Indicators* report contains data going back to 1950. It is extremely useful for history papers concerning social and economic issues involving young adults.

ZIPSKINNY.COM

URL Address: http://zipskinny.com/
  Site Summary: Begin by entering a ZIP code or choosing a community within a selected state to use this census-based data site. It provides a plethora of social, economic, and demographic indicators that yield a statistical snapshot of towns and cities throughout the United States. Students can access the data to compare various cities' or towns' educational achievement levels with others. One can determine how many of a town's or city's citizens live above or below the poverty line and even how stable a community is by the length of time people have lived in their homes. History students can enter ZIP codes to discover how communities have changed or not changed over time and explore the possible causes.

Critical Thinking Questions and Activities

1. The area where the "Dust Bowl" occurred in the 1930s was settled in the late 1800s by farmers who uprooted the native prairie grass to grow wheat. When the bottom fell out of the wheat market, many lost their farms and left the land fallow. The subsequent drought and constantly blowing winds created enormous destructive dust storms that further devastated the area in town and cities such as Dalhart, TX (79034), Boise City, OK (73933), and Rolla, KS (67954). Enter these ZIP codes individually into the search box. How have these areas fared since the 1930s from a social, demographic, and economic standpoint? Look at the "population density" data. This area was once known as "No-Man's Land." What should it be termed now?

2. The area known as "Silicon Valley" is located in and around California's third largest city, San Jose. It experienced rapid growth in the high-tech and electronics fields when companies such as Cisco, Adobe Systems, IBM, and eBay began to employ large numbers of workers. Insert the zip codes 95102, 95103, 95106, 95108, 95139, 95118, 95141, 95142, and 95148, and note the results. How would you describe the educational levels of these areas? Do most of the people have some college education? If one wished to live in Silicon Valley, what skills and education might you need to thrive?

3. Can a ZIP code increase your chances for being a victim of a crime? The 2011 Federal Bureau of Investigation's ten most dangerous cities included Baltimore, Detroit, and Memphis on its list. Yet all of these cities are frequented by tourists and workers without much mishap. Each city, however, is on the list because of specific areas where the crime rate is unusually high. The old Palmer Avenue section of Detroit, MI (48202), the Front Street neighborhood of Baltimore, MD (21202), and the Lamar Avenue area of Memphis, TN (38114), are where most of the crime occurs. Use the "Compare ZIP codes" part of the site and insert these ZIP codes. Compare the resulting data. What do these areas of each city have in common demographically, socially, and economically? How do they compare to other ZIP codes in the same cities? If you were the mayor of one of these cities, what steps would you take to reduce crime based on the statistical portrait of the crime-ridden areas?

4. In 2012, the top five poorest cities in America were Detroit, MI, Buffalo, NY, Cincinnati, OH, Cleveland, OH, and Miami, FL. Enter these respective ZIP codes into the "Compare ZIP codes" search box. What statistical variables do these cities have in common that probably contribute to their poverty? What effect do these rankings have on the people living in these cities?

Related Internet Sites

County Demographics
www.geolytics.com/CountyDemographics
Provides information concerning population, race, educational attainment, employment, and housing values that is similar to ZIPskinny.com.
ZIP Code Lookup
www.brainzip.com
Browsable by state and ZIP codes, this site also furnishes users with demographic information about millions of towns and cities in the United States.

NOTE

1. Cohen, B., & Greenfield, J. (1998). *Ben & Jerry's double-dip: How to run a values-led business and make money, too*. New York: Simon & Schuster, p. 222.

Chapter Four

U.S. History Sites

ALL ABOUT CALIFORNIA AND THE INDUCEMENTS TO SETTLE THERE (1870)

URL Address: http://archive.org/details/allaboutcaliforn00cali
Site Summary: Within two years of President Polk announcing that gold had been discovered in California in 1948, it became a state. By 1869, the transcontinental railroad was completed and began transporting people and agricultural and manufactured products from east to west. The railroad was a hugely profitable businesses for central Pacific major investors such as Leland Stanford and Mark Hopkins, but only if the state was sufficiently populated to make use of their railroad.

In 1870, along with other wealthy businessmen, they formed the California Immigrant Union, which touted the natural resources and opportunities of California to encourage people to migrate west. This site contains the original report that's filled with data about California's potential for homesteading, employment, travel, and pleasure.

Critical Thinking Questions and Activities

1. Scroll to page nineteen and note the table about "Rates of Wages." Find the top paying five occupations. On page twenty-one of the report, it states that "the Chinamen perfect themselves in any department of business" and work "willingly for 75 cents to $1.00 per day." Why were the Chinese paid less, and what effect might this have had on wages being paid to the top five occupations? Discuss how this disparity might cause bad animosity among workers competing for the same jobs.

2. Scroll to pages forty-two and forty-three, "Total Area of California," and study the part of the table showing the total number of acres in California. What percentage of California's acreage was "claimed by the railroads"? In a short paper, discuss the implications for the railroads owning so much land and their potential for dominant, political power within the state.
3. Scroll to page fifty-two, "Square Miles and Population." Why do the authors of the report claim that California has the capacity to accommodate more than twelve million people? Was this estimate an exaggeration for the time period or was it an accurate assessment?
4. Scroll to page sixty-five and note the table showing "the number of children between the ages of 5 and 15 years in the five most populous counties." What was the ratio of children to the number of schools in these counties? The report sings the praises of California's school system. Do your own ratio calculations reinforce this statement or cause you to question the assertion?

Related Internet Sites

California As I Saw It: First Person Narratives of California's Early Years (1849–1900)
  http://rs6.loc.gov/amhome.html
  Contains 190 eyewitness accounts of California that can be used to verify many of the statements in the *California Immigrant Union Report*.
Mining History and Geology of the Mother Lode
  http://virtual.yosemite.cc.ca.us/ghayes/goldrush.htm
  Provides geological information about how to mine gold, but more importantly, what the environmental effects were on California during the gold rush.

AMERICAN SOLDIER SURVEYS OF WORLD WAR II

URL Address:
http://www.ropercenter.uconn.edu/dta_access/data/datasets/ams.html
  Site Summary: Soon after the Japanese attack on Pearl Harbor, the War Department began surveying soldiers in the U.S. armed services so the army could obtain information that would assist them in establishing policies and procedures. The scope and legacy of these surveys is enormous since the army polled more than half a million soldiers. The subjects ranged from questions about their living conditions and entertainment preferences to inquiries about their feelings concerning combat and attitudes towards the enemy. This treasure trove of data can be employed by history and social

sciences students and extrapolated for changes over time regarding current armed conflicts that the United States is presently involved.

Critical Thinking Questions and Activities

1. Record the responses to five survey questions concerning "The Attitudes of Enlisted Men Toward the Army—Part B" and "The Attitudes of Officers Towards the Army—Part B." Design a bar graph showing the differences in responses to the same questions by each group. Why do you think enlisted men felt differently than officers did about being in the Armed Services?
2. Click on the survey "Attitudes Toward Radio Programs." Letters from home were one way of getting the news, but most of it was local. The main way soldiers received news was by listening to the radio. Read the responses to the survey questions regarding use of the radio for news broadcasts. Imagine that you have just been appointed as a communications officer for a brigade of soldiers. What new programs and broadcasts would you feature based on the soldiers' responses. How frequently would you broadcast the news?
3. Click on the survey "Reactions to the Enemy and Further Duty." A total of 1,232 of the men surveyed reported being in "actual combat" and 413 reported being "under combat fire." Compute the responses regarding "troubled by hands sweating," "upset stomach," "sleeping," and "bothered by nervousness" into percentages. What percentage of these soldiers seem to have experienced some form of post-traumatic stress syndrome? Compare this percentage to those of soldiers who have served in Iraq and Afghanistan. Did you find similarities or dissimilarities? What would you do to reduce these numbers if the United States were to engage in a future armed conflict?
4. Click on the survey on page two entitled "Attitudes of Hospital Patients Toward Medical Care." What percentage of patients were hospitalized for wounds received in combat? What percentage were hospitalized for other reasons? What seems to be the main reason that soldiers were hospitalized? If you were a medical planner in World War II, what types of doctors (surgeons, general practitioners, or other specialists) would you staff your hospitals with based on these responses? Research some of the illnesses that soldiers suffered from during World War II. What could the Armed Services have done to prevent them?

Related Internet Sites

A Brief History of the U.S. Army in World War II

http://www.history.army.mil/brochures/brief/overview.htm
Although this site does not contain much quantitative data, it does have short summaries of individual battles and campaigns for students who may not be familiar with World War II.

U.S. Army Divisions in World War II
http://www.historyshots.com/usarmy/backstory.cfm
Packed with data concerning troop strength for various battles and campaigns, numbers of casualties in various battles, and days of combat for different campaigns, this site can be used for several different types of quantitative data assignments.

BIOWAR

URL Address: http://www.gwu.edu/~nsarchiv/NSAEBB/NSAEBB58/
Site Summary: In 1969, President Richard M. Nixon decided to cease building an offensive biological and chemical weapons program. His decision was influenced by public outcry at the use of Agent Orange, a poisonous herbicide that was sprayed over jungle areas during the Vietnam War to defoliate it. President Nixon submitted the 1925 Geneva Protocol, which would ban biological and chemical weapons, to the Senate for ratification, and in 1972 joined more than one hundred nations in signing the Biological and Toxin Weapons Convention. The latter agreement banned possession of biological weapons with the exception of those developed for defensive purposes. Although most of the twenty-six documents lack quantitative data, two of them contain chilling lists of expenditures and inventories of these highly dangerous substances and weapons and reveal the past and, perhaps, present extent of the U.S. biological weapons program.

Critical Thinking Questions and Activities

1. Open "Document 6A" and scroll to pages eleven to thirteen. Create a table that displays U.S. biological and chemical weapons capabilities based upon the stockpiled amounts in the 1960s. Use these figures to argue that these weapons are inherently dangerous to stockpile and may be excessive given the U.S. nuclear weapons program.

2. Open "Document 6A" and scroll to page fourteen. Note the chemical program costs for fiscal year 1970 (FY70) funding. Scroll to page sixteen and note the costs of the biological programs. Why was the biological program less costly than the chemical weapons program? Employ the data to persuade President Richard M. Nixon that these programs should no longer be funded and that the funds could be used for other purposes.

3. Open "Document 26" and scroll to pages 80 to 101. Extract the names of colleges and universities from the list that had research and development biological and chemical weapons contracts with the U.S. Government. Which universities and colleges had the most government contracts? Why do you suppose this was? Discuss the ethical implications of higher education institutions assisting the government in the development of biological and chemical weapons. What moral laws do you feel they might have violated?

4. Open "Document 26" and scroll to pages 124 to 142. Read through the lists of tests performed in the military and public domains on animals, crops, and humans. Employ the data as evidence to show the actual and potential deadly effects of these biological agents. Imagine that you are a journalist for a major newspaper. Cite the most salient data in a written exposé about the biological and chemical weapons tests performed by the U.S. Government upon innocent civilians and U.S. public areas.

Related Internet Sites

Biological Weapons and International Humanitarian Law
http://www.icrc.org/
This site sponsored by the International Committee of the Red Cross provides a series of links with current information about the status of biological weapons throughout the world.

World Health Organization Public Health Response to Biological and Chemical Weapons
http://www.who.int/csr/delibepidemics/en/allchapspreliminaries_may03.pdf
Scroll to the Appendices of this site to obtain embedded data about all the major biological and chemical attacks since 1970, including the 1995 sarin nerve gas attacks in the Tokyo subway and the U.S. postal anthrax attacks in 2001.

THE BISBEE DEPORTATION (1917)

URL Address: http://www.library.arizona.edu/exhibits/bisbee/
Site Summary: Many events in American history are reflective of their political climate. The Bisbee deportation that transpired during World War I was one of them. On July 12, 1917, approximately 1,300 striking copper miners, their advocates, and numerous innocent observers were loaded onto filthy cattle cars in Bisbee, AZ, by two thousand armed vigilantes. The vigilantes were under the supervision of Walter S. Douglas, who was president of the Phelps Dodge copper mine. They were hauled two hundred miles

away in stifling heat to Hermanas, NM, with orders never to return. Mr. Phelp's vigilantes continued to impose martial law on Bisbee, preventing many citizens from returning to their homes until November 1917 when a presidential labor commission declared the entire operation in violation of both state and federal laws.

Critical Thinking Questions and Activities

1. Under "Resources," click on "Articles" and read the article titled "Gaining a Foothold in the Paradise of Capitalism." Click back to the heading "Deportees." With the exception of the Mexicans who were not allowed to work underground and who were used as strikebreakers, all the deportees were white. Employ the nationalities data to show how this common factor facilitated organizing the workers into the Western Federation of Miners.
2. Under "History," click on "Reports" and read the report titled "Mining Conditions in Bisbee, Arizona." Examine the sliding pay scale data showing how much the copper miners and muckers were paid relative to the price of copper set by the government during World War I. Compare their pay to the list of current prices on staple groceries listed on the same page. Discuss the fairness or unfairness of the miners' pay as a factor in their subsequent strike.
3. Many of the deportees were characterized by Walter Douglas and his managers as foreign agitators with possible ties to Germany. Under the heading "Deportees," analyze how the data concerning their citizenship and purchase of Liberty bonds may refute that allegation.
4. Under "Primary Resources," select "Reports" and click on the link "Mining Conditions in Bisbee, Arizona." Note the wages that the copper miners were being paid and the table showing the cost of groceries. Research the profits that the copper companies were reaping during World War I. Write a muckraking article arguing that the miners were being exploited during this time and deserved to share more in the company's windfall.

Related Internet Sites

Jerome Deportation (Precursor to the Bisbee Deportation)
  http://www.azjerome.com/pages/jerome/wobblies.htm
Provides information about a previous deportation of miners in Jerome, AZ, which helped generate the idea for the Bisbee deportation.
Union-busting at Cripple Creek
  http://historymatters.gmu.edu/d/5654/d/5653/

Supplies primary source evidence of a similar deportation of miners at a mine in Cripple Creek, CO.

COAL MINING IN THE GILDED AGE AND PROGRESSIVE ERA

URL Address: http://ehistory.osu.edu/osu/mmh/gildedage/

Site Summary: Coal mining has always been a hazardous occupation, but in the nineteenth century it was particularly dangerous because the technology had not been developed to consistently mine coal at depths of 1,500 feet into the Earth. Workers, many of them children, labored under conditions that were unsafe and for wages that barely enabled them to subsist. This collection of coal mining links from the Ohio State University History Collection contains quantitative data about the extent of coal mining in Ohio, Pennsylvania, New York, and Delaware. The data is useful for exploring the causes and effects of the great coal strikes that occurred during the time of the "Coal Barons," and how the use of coal as a source of energy and steel production has changed over time.

Critical Thinking Questions and Activities

1. Click on the link "How important was coal mining to the American economy?" and examine the graph titled "Index 1967." Juxtapose the peaks when coal production was the highest with a timeline of historical events. Analyze how these events affected the price of coal during this time, and research what corresponding wages were allotted for coal miners.

2. Click on the link "Machines and the Coal Miner's Work." New technologies unleash what some historians call "creative destruction." In other words, they sometimes eliminate some jobs and occupations while similarly creating new ones. Use the data that is available in the links "How extensive was mechanized coal mining over time?" and "What was the impact of increased mine mechanization?" to illustrate this syndrome. Compare it to the invention of the personal computer and the demise of the electric typewriter.

3. Click the link "The Anthracite Coal Strike" followed by the link "The Real Issue of the Coal Strike." Extract the embedded data from this article. Use it to create a short graphic story or series of empathetic cartoons depicting the life of a coal miner for publication in a muckraking magazine.

4. Click on the link "Anthracite Coal Mines and Mining." Scroll to the section "Controlling the Output." Use the data to show how the coal company owners were mutually engaged in ensuring that the price of

coal remained high despite the fact that there was a surplus of avail-
ably mined coal. Can you make any comparisons to the present-day oil
and gas industry?

Related Internet Sites

The Coal Strike of 1902—Turning Point in U.S. Policy
http://www.dol.gov/oasam/prorams/history
Provides an excellent overview of the anthracite coal strike and its impact
on the American labor movement. It also contains general data in the form of
the number of workers and strikers involved.
Coal Production Data Files
http://histclo.com/act/work/slave/ast/ast-atle.html
Provides statistics about coal production in the United States from 1991
to 2008. A second section includes production projections through 2014.

COLD WAR AIR DEFENSE RELIED ON WIDESPREAD DISPERSAL OF NUCLEAR WEAPONS

**URL Address: http://www.gwu.edu/~nsarchiv/nukevault/et (get rest of
address)**
Site Summary: The Cold War was raging by the 1950s when the Union
of Soviet Socialist Republics (USSR) and the United States were vying to see
who could accumulate the most nuclear weapons to counteract a hypothetical
attack by the other side. Intercontinental ballistic missiles had not been produced. Under the auspices of President Dwight D. Eisenhower and congress,
the United States embarked upon a program of dispersing nuclear weapons
throughout the states as a means of destroying attacking USSR planes and
the bombs they carried while creating minimal damage to the populace. This
site provides quantitative data about the numbers of nuclear weapons that
were deployed and shows how U.S. reliance upon protocol-based plans
placed the public at grave risk during the Cuban Missile Crisis.

Critical Thinking Questions and Activities

1. On the homepage of the site, note the data about the number of rockets
   and missiles that were deployed throughout the United States beginning in 1957. Display the data in a scattergram so that a citizen could
   understand the extent and scope of the deployments.
2. Click on "Document 4, Weapon Costs Revealed." Read the short address by Colonel Barney Oldfield, public information officer for the
   Continental Air Defense Command. What was the cost of the Genie

rocket? Use this information and the numbers of rockets that were cited on the homepage of this site to calculate what the costs of the Genie rockets were to American taxpayers. Why was Colonel Oldfield reprimanded for releasing this information? Was this information that the American public was entitled to have in the public record during that time or should it have remained a secret?

3. Under the heading "The Nuclear Vault," click on the link "Special Collection: Key Documents on Nuclear Weapons Policy 1949-1990." Scroll to number "3c Presentation by the Strategic Air Command, Commanders Conference, Ramey Air Force Base, 25-26-27 April 1950." Read pages nine to fourteen of the report. How many of the bombers that are referred to in the report are equipped with atomic weapons? Research the political situation with the USSR in 1950. Write a pro and con memo to President Dwight D. Eisenhower concerning the numbers of U.S. bombers that carried atomic weapons since 1945.

4. Under the heading "Nuclear Vault," click on the link "Letter from General George C. Kenney, Air University, to Air Force Chief of Staff General Hoyt S. Vandenberg, 29 April 1950." As the rhetoric between the USSR and the United States escalated during the Cold War, General George C. Kenney wrote a report to General Hoyt S. Vandenberg arguing for a "first strike" against the USSR. Extract General Kenney's estimates of the USSR's readiness for war and that of the United States and create a table displaying each estimate. Imagine that you are President Dwight D. Eisenhower. Describe how you would have responded in writing to this proposal about a first strike.

Related Internet Sites

The Nuclear Vault
http://www.gwu.edu/~nsarchiv/nukevault/index.htm
Students can refer to this site for additional quantitative material regarding the Cold War and use of nuclear weapons.

Web-Based Primary Sources for Nuclear History
http://nuclearsecrecy.com/blog/2011/11/14/web-based-primary-sources-for-nuclear-history/
Provides a list of the most relevant web sites for historical research about nuclear weapons. Many of them contain quantitative data and can be used for tracing changes over time and making comparisons among decades.

THE CYCLOPEDIA OF TEMPERANCE, PROHIBITION, AND PUBLIC MORALS

URL   Address: http://books.google.com/bkshp?hl=en&tab=wp   (Type book title in search box.)

Site Summary: From the 1840s through 1920, a major reform movement, partially fueled by the religious fervor of evangelical Protestant denominations, began publishing tracts filled with statistics about the evils of alcohol. Their goal was to achieve passage of the eighteenth amendment to the Constitution that banned the sale, manufacture, and transportation of alcohol. This A to Z encyclopedia published by the authority of the Methodist Episcopal Church is filled with quantitative data about the brewing industry, growth of saloons, and other information that shows the zeal with which various pro-prohibition groups went about proselytizing the public with the hope of passing the amendment.

Critical Thinking Questions and Activities

1. Read pages nine to sixteen under the heading "Advertising of Liquors." The prohibition movement placed a great deal of pressure on newspapers that accepted advertisements from liquor stores or manufacturers. Review the tabulated data noting the states listing the number of newspapers within them that declined liquor advertising. If you were an advocate for prohibition, which states' newspapers would you target for increased pressure and why?

2. Read pages thirty to thirty-one under the heading "Arkansas." Review the tabulated data results concerning the period that Arkansas was "with saloons" versus "without saloons." Employ the data to develop modern graphs to support a case for the passage of the eighteenth amendment.

3. Read pages forty to forty-seven under the heading "Beer." Review the data that is cited about the production of beer, especially in the United States. Employ the data to show the correlation between the increase in beer production and the technological changes brought about by the telegraph, railroads, and mechanical refrigeration. Refer to the following site, called *Temperance & Prohibition*, for additional data: http://prohibition.osu.edu/saloons/study-great-immoralities.

4. Read pages eighty-seven to eighty-eight under the heading "Cities." As the prohibition movement gained momentum, more states banned alcohol before the passage of the eighteenth amendment. These states were known as "dry" states versus "wet." Analyze the data displayed on pages eighty-seven and eighty-eight. If you were a traveling Methodist pastor proselytizing against alcohol, which states and their re-

spective cities would you seek to convert next? Explain why you would choose those states based on the existing data.

Related Internet Sites

The Ram's Horn: An Interdenominational Social Gospel Magazine
http://ehistory.osu.edu/osu/mmh/Rams_Horn/
Published in the 1890s, issues of this pro-prohibition magazine feature articles about the liquor industry and prohibition that are similar to the *Cyclopedia of Temperance, Prohibition and Public Morals.*

Temperance & Prohibition
http://prohibition.osu.edu/saloons/study-great-immoralities
An excellent site with additional quantitative data linking the increase in the beer industry and saloon growth to advances in transportation and improvements with refrigeration.

THE DOMESTIC SLAVE TRADE

URL Address: http://www.inmotionaame.org/migrations/
Site Summary: In 1807, Congress abolished the importation of slaves into the United States. While it ended the legal shipment of slaves to America's shores, it did nothing to stop the domestic slave trade from flourishing right up until the Civil War in 1861. The reason for this robust market in the purchasing and selling of human beings was purely economic. Most of the country's business was agricultural in nature, and human labor was still a necessity for planting, growing, and harvesting crops. In the South, cotton was a booming crop and plantation owners were eager to purchase slaves to work the fields and keep their production costs as low as possible.

An extensive market developed in the sale and transportation of slaves from northern states to southern states and among southern states. The sale of people reaped vast profits for so many traders that domestic slavery was considered a market similar to the industrial ones in the twentieth century. It was characterized by rising and falling prices, speculation, and auctions. This site contains background information about the domestic slave trade along with links to primary sources featuring census data and other statistics about the economic aspects of this "peculiar institution" known as slavery.

Critical Thinking Questions and Activities

1. Select "Exporters and Importers" and click on the link "Slavery and the Internal Slave Trade in the United States of America." Scroll to pages four and five of the data and study the tabulated data. How

would you describe the domestic slave trade as a market based on the 1810, 1820, and 1830 census data?

2. Study "Table III" on page seven. How did slaves fare demographically in comparison to whites and "free coloreds" from 1800 to 1830? What conclusions can you draw about the domestic slave market based on these figures?

3. Study "Table IV" on pages eight and nine. Find the top five states that experienced the greatest increase in their slave population from 1790 to 1830. What factors, with the exception of the need for workers in the cotton fields, do you attribute the increase?

4. Select "Exporters and Importers," and click on the link "Slavery and the Internal Slave Trade in the United States of America." Read page thirteen about the overall profits to be made from domestic slave trading. Return to "Exporters and Importers," and click on the link "The Domestic Slave trade in Mississippi and the Forks of the Road Slave Market at Natchez." Read page eight about slave prices.

   Use the data to create an economic profile of this market. If you were an economist charged with abolishing it not by law but by waging economic war, how would you proceed? Hint: The prices of slaves seem to fluctuate with the rise and fall of cotton prices. Might you suggest a national boycott of non-essential cotton goods produced by slave labor?

Related Internet Sites

The Domestic Slave Trade in America: The Lifeblood of the Southern Slave System
   http://www.inmotionaame.org/migrations/topic.cfm?migration=3&topic=1&tab=image
   This site contains some quantitative data, but more importantly it explains how the system operated from an economic perspective. It is useful for answering questions 1 and 4.

Slavery in Virginia: A Selected Bibliography
   http://www.lva.virginia.gov/public/guides/SlaveryInVA.pdf
   The first page of this selected bibliography provides a census-sourced table with a ranking of the top slave-holding states and the numbers of slaves in each of those states.

THE DROUGHT OF 1934

**URL Address: http://fraser.stlouisfed.org/docs/publications/
   books/drought _1934_aaa.pdf**

Site Summary: In the 1930s, the entire Great Plains as well as neighboring states experienced insufficient rainfall for almost a decade. The ensuing drought, economic conditions of the Great Depression, and the blinding dust storms generated by soil erosion combined to make areas of Kansas, Colorado, New Mexico, and Texas almost uninhabitable. In Boise, OK, for example, an average of less than twelve inches of rain fell per year from 1931 to 1936. In response to the poverty and environmental devastation caused by these twin perils, President Franklin D. Roosevelt tasked a Drought Committee with providing financial, agricultural, and other forms of assistance. The subsequent report contains tabulated data about relief efforts, financial aid, and other basic drought solution operations.

Critical Thinking Questions and Activities

1. Scroll to page seventeen of the report and view "Table 1." Explain why the percentages in this table are somewhat deceptive for the Dust Bowl states, including Nebraska, Oklahoma, Kansas, New Mexico, and Texas. Why do the percentages fail to reveal the dire situation for these drought states? Research wind speed, soil erosion, normal rainfall in these states, staple crops, and moisture content of the soil before formulating your answer.

2. Scroll to pages twenty-two and twenty-three of the report and view "Table 2" and "Table 3." Which states show more serious crop conditions? What natural weather conditions in these states make them more vulnerable to a serious drought in comparison to other surrounding states?

3. Scroll to page forty-two of the report. Note the amount of relief funds allocated from the total $475,000,000 available. The fifth item on the list allots fifty million dollars for the emergency purchase of submarginal farms and assistance in re-locating families. Which states would you target for re-location and why?

4. Scroll to page forty-five of the report and view "Table 5." Why were so few of the Dust Bowl states included under "emergency status" in 1934? Should the government have been able to foresee that conditions would worsen dramatically in the coming years based on previous years of weather data?

Related Internet Sites

Historical PDSI Graphs by River Basin
http://drought.unl.edu/Planning/Monitoring/HistoricalPDSIMaps/ HistoricalPDSIGraphs.aspx

Contains graphs regarding droughts for all of the major river basins in and around the Dust Bowl back to 1895.

Surviving the Dust Bowl

http://www.pbs.org/wgbh/americanexperience/features/general-article/dustbowl-mass-exodus-plains/

Provides embedded quantitative data about the number of people and states affected by the Dust Bowl and numbers of persons who relocated to other states.

HISTORICAL CENSUS DATA BROWSER 1790–1970

URL Address: http://mapserver.lib.virginia.edu/

Site Summary: Students can find it challenging to manipulate the variables in census data. The collected data of the U.S. Census from 1790 to 1960 are already summarized on this site so that users can easily select sets of population and economic variables for analysis and interpretation. Students can choose ten-year intervals from 1790 to 1960 for each state and county. The database also contains tables for displaying, sorting, printing, and graphing the results. Within the year 1860, for example, students have a choice of categories, including free colored population, slave population, white population, education, literacy, marriage, and births and deaths. Within these categories are drop-down menus that support further delineation by age, gender, and so on.

Critical Thinking Questions and Activities

1. Select the census years 1790 to 1850. For each year, select the variable "total number of slaves." Click on "graph states." Note the demographic patterns that emerge as you graph each census year. What states are experiencing the largest gains in slave population? Which state has the most states for the census year 1850? Research this factor and each state's position on slavery.
2. Select the 1850 census year and choose the variable "total no. of white adults who cannot read or write." What states have the highest illiteracy rates? What states have the lowest rates? What conditions may have accounted for these rates? Be sure to look at patterns of immigration in those particular states for that particular period of time.
3. Select the 1870 census year and choose the variable "no. persons born in Ireland." What states have the largest numbers of people who were born in Ireland? What event in Ireland prior to 1850 helped contribute to this demographic distribution?

4. Select the 1960 census year and choose the variable "no. of persons of foreign stock reporting Ireland (Eire) as country of origin." What states have the largest numbers of people who were born in Ireland?

Related Internet Sites

U.S. Census Bureau Help Using Our Web Site and Data
http://www.census.gov/main/www/help.html
Features a useful frequently asked questions section and contact links for specific census-related questions.

U.S. Census Bureau
http://www.census.gov
Contains the homepage for all U.S. Census information. Several links are especially suited to secondary school students.

HOW MANY NUKES AND WHERE ARE THE NUKES?

URL Address: http://www.gwu.edu/~nsarchiv/NSAEBB/NSAEBB197/index.htm

Site Summary: During the Cold War (1950 to 1990), the U.S. Government embarked upon a nuclear arms race with the Soviet Union. Both countries manufactured and deployed thousands of nuclear weapons around the world, each within its relative spheres of influence. The United States deployed thirteen thousand nuclear weapons outside the country, with most of them installed in Germany, Italy, Belgium, and Great Britain. Their deployment was so secret that even the U.S. Congress experienced problems obtaining information about their quantity and placement. This site at the National Security Archive contains documents that had been de-classified for decades and now have been re-classified for security reasons. The document variants showing the new redactions in the data make for fascinating research and critical thinking questions concerning the U.S. nuclear defense program.

Critical Thinking Questions and Activities

1. Scroll down to "Part I–Numbers," and click on "Variant A: Declassified 1999." Read through pages one to eight of the document. Click on "Variant B: Declassified 2006" and examine the same page numbers. What data in "Variant B" has the government chosen to reclassify. Why have Pentagon officials elected to redact the data that was available in 1999? What is the possible military vulnerability of the data?

2. Scroll down to "Part I–Numbers," and click on "Document 3." Explain how and why the United States could "spin" the data displaying strategic nuclear weapons superiority either in favor of the United States or the Soviet Union. Why would the U.S. Department of Defense choose to spin the numbers? Be sure to include such possibilities as arguing in favor of arms control, in favor of an increase in defense department spending, or some other military policy.
3. Scroll to "Documents 2A–C." Compare the data for the U.S. nuclear stockpile in the "1966, 1967, and 1969 U.S. Department of Defense Annual Reports." What patterns in terms of increases or decreases are present in the embedded data? Why did the Pentagon choose to make this data non-classified and readily available to the public in the 1960s? Research what the Soviet Union's public position on arms control was during this period.
4. Scroll to "Documents 4A and B." Study the chart in "Document 4A" that numerically shows national security strategic defense policies, expenditures, and numbers of deployable nuclear weapons under the Eisenhower, Kennedy-Johnson, and Nixon administrations. Notice that portions of the chart have been redacted. Click on "Document 4B" and study the un-redacted portion of the chart. Based upon the data, what is your assessment of U.S. readiness for the various listed contingencies during this time period? How might the data that is displayed on this portion of the chart affect present national security? Do you think that it is too sensitive to be de-classified?

Related Internet Sites

What Nuclear Weapons Cost Us
   http://www.ploughshares.org/what-nuclear-weapons-cost-us
   In addition to well-displayed statistics and data, this site contains a complete downloadable PDF report about the budget-draining costs of nuclear weapons.
World Nuclear Stockpile Report
   http://www.ploughshares.org/world-nuclear-stockpile-report
   This site, also from the Plough Shares organization, provides contemporary data and statistics about the estimated nuclear weapons that each of the nine publicly acknowledged countries with nuclear arms possesses.

ILLINOIS CENTRAL RAILROAD AND ITS COLONIZATION WORK

URL Address: http://ocp.hul.harvard.edu/immigration/ (In the search box, type in the site title.)

Site Summary: After completion of the Erie Canal in 1825 and several railroads in the 1830s, almost every state embarked on series state and federally funded internal improvement projects designed to allow their citizens' products to be transported more quickly and easily as well as to encourage people to settle within their states. Illinois was no exception. In 1851, Illinois became the first land grant railroad, receiving a grant from President Millard Fillmore to construct a railroad that would eventually connect Chicago, IL, to New Orleans, LA, and Mobile, AL, and build branches reaching Omaha, NB, Fort Dodge, IO, and Sioux Falls, ND.

State politicians and railroad financiers immediately realized that Illinois lacked the population to support the size and scale of their business interests, so they set about attracting immigrants to the state with advertisements, paid travel accounts by visitors, and other enticements. The Harvard Immigration site contains a 1934 book by George Wallace Gates with interesting data that demonstrates the nineteenth-century colonization work performed by the railroads.

Critical Thinking Questions and Activities

1. Click on page 217 and read the advertisement "Homes for the Industrious." Does all of the data about the land, etc., ring true to you? What parts of the advertisement would you question if you were a potential land buyer?

2. Click on pages 240 and 241. The Illinois Central Railroad had acquired large holdings of land in the central and eastern parts of the state. Extract the data on these pages and create a table showing how successful the company's agents were by 1856 in increasing the population or colonizing these parts of Illinois. Explain why it was in their interest to populate these areas of Illinois in detail. Discuss what the political implications were for the 1856 and 1860 presidential elections.

3. Click on page 260 and note the statistics displayed in "Table 1. Statistics Relating to the Land Sales of the Illinois Central." Employ the data to show how the sale of Illinois Central Railroad lands was a reflection of the economic conditions of the period.

4. Click on page 261 and note the statistics displayed in "Table 2. Number of Land Sales and Cancellations Per Unit." During the mid-1850s, it was obvious that a civil war might be about to occur. What socioeconomic and political factors may have accounted for the continued high sale of Illinois land during these years and even during the Civil War?

Related Internet Sites

Illinois Central Historical Society
http://icrrhistorical.org/history.html
Features a map showing the main routes and all branches of the Illinois Central Railroad plus a brief overview of its history.

Immigration, Railroads, and the West
http://ocp.hul.harvard.edu/immigration/railroads.html
Harvard University supports an extensive database of texts, photos, and other documents about the transformative role that immigrants have played in the industrial and agricultural development of the United States. Many of the links on this web site contain embedded quantitative data and tabulated statistics.

IN THE FOOTSTEPS OF LEWIS AND CLARK, U.S. POPULATION GROWTH

URL Address: http://blog.oup.com/2012/05/lewis-clark-expedition-us-population-growth/

Site Summary: In 1803, President Thomas Jefferson, with the purpose of "extending the external commerce of the United States," requested $2,500 from Congress to finance an expedition into the West. To lead the trip, President Jefferson chose his private secretary Meriwether Lewis to not only explore uncharted territory but also serve as the group's resident botanist, zoologist, geographer, and negotiator with Native Americans. Mr. Lewis selected fellow Virginian and Indian Wars veteran William Clark to share the administrative burdens. Their meticulous journals filled with the beauty and excitement of their 3,700 mile journey challenged and tantalized Americans who were eager to expand to the West. This interactive site provides statistics in an artfully displayed manner to show history students the tremendous impact that this expedition had on populating the West.

Critical Thinking and Activities

1. Study the census data and corresponding maps for the following census years: 1810, 1820, 1830, 1840, 1850, 1860, and 1870. How closely do the population increases reflect the route taken by Lewis and Clark?
2. By the 1810 census, America's population "had increased by 36% from 5.3 to 7.2 million."What world events besides the Lewis and Clark expedition also contributed to this increase?
3. Study the 1840 and 1850 censuses. Most states show a pattern of being declared a territory and then eventually becoming a state. The

exception on these census maps is California. Research the economic and political conditions that enabled California to skip this pattern and move directly to statehood.

4. Click on the 1860 census. Note that a portion of the United States is called "Indian territory." Click on the 1870 census. What state has replaced "Indian territory"? Discuss how population density may have played a role along with other factors in changing this designation from a territory to a state.

Related Internet Sites

The U.S. Westward Expansion
http://economics.ucr.edu/seminars/fall06/ets/Vandenbroucke12-4-06.pdf
This paper about expansion of the West by Guillaume Vandenbroucke is filled with population data and other statistics concerning the probable reasons and motivations for such dramatic demographic changes in the United States during the mid-nineteenth century.

Westward Expansion
http://www.smithsoniansource.org/display/topic/viewdetailshis.aspx?TopicId=1000
The Smithsonian Institution site contains several data-based questions about the impact that westward expansion had upon Native Americans during the mid-nineteenth century.

THE INFLUENZA EPIDEMIC OF 1928 TO 1929 WITH COMPARATIVE DATA FOR 1918 TO 1919

URL Address: http://www.ncbi.nlm.nih.gov/pmc/articles/PMC1555806/pdf/amjphnation00618-0019.pdf

Site Summary: Just as World War I (1914–1918) was drawing to a close, having cost the lives of an estimated fifty million people, a strain of influenza emerged that killed at least another forty million people worldwide. It was so virulent that many people died overnight from the effects of high fever and a suffocating pneumonia. It was most deadly for persons between twenty and forty years old. In the United States, 28 percent of the population was infected and in the end, 675,000 Americans died from it. This site contains a 1930 article published in the *American Journal of Public Health* and *The Nation's Health* by Selwyn D. Collins, Ph.D. It is replete with comparative statistics, graphs, and charts about two major influenza epidemics.

Critical Thinking Questions and Activities

1. Scroll to page 121 of the article and note the statistics displayed in "Table 1." Which areas of the country had the highest number of deaths under the column labeled 1920? What cities are located in those regions, and what are their populations? Examine the relationship between cities where large numbers of soldiers were either embarking or disembarking from the World War I front, as well as their death rates. What are your conclusions?
2. Scroll to page 23 of the article and note the statistics displayed in "Figure III." Employ the statistics to argue that the rapid spread of influenza in 1918 to 1919 may have hindered the government response to it.
3. Scroll to page 126 of the article and note the graph results displayed in "Figure IV." New London, CT, experienced many more deaths in the 1918 to 1919 pandemic than did other cities that were surveyed. What role may World War I have played in this high death rate? (Hint: Was this city where many soldiers were returning from Europe?)
4. Scroll to page 128 of the article and note the graph displayed in "Figure V." What ages were most vulnerable to the 1918 to 1919 influenza pandemic? Discuss what the effects of the pandemic probably had on the U.S. economy.

Related Internet Sites

The Economic Effects of the 1918 Influenza Epidemic
  http://birdflubook.org/resources/brainerd1.pdf
  Contains quantitative data about the effects of the 1918 influenza pandemic on the U.S. economy.
Pandemic Economics: The 1918 Influenza and Its Modern-Day Implications
  http://www.nmhealth.org/documents/
PandemiceconomicsFedReserveBank0308.pdf
  Provides a March/April 2008 article published in the *Federal Reserve Bank of St. Louis Review* by Thomas A. Garrett that is filled with tabulated data about the effects of the 1918 influenza pandemic on the United States in 1918.

LEND-LEASE SHIPMENTS: WORLD WAR II

URL Address: http://www.ibiblio.org/hyperwar/USA/ref/LL-Ship/LL-Ship-1.html

Site Summary: The Lend-Lease Act, passed by the U.S. Congress in March 1941, officially empowered President Franklin D. Roosevelt to loan billions of dollars' worth of military equipment, weapons, planes, and transportation and communications equipment to Great Britain, the Soviet Union, Free France, and China. The equipment was technically "loaned" in exchange for leasing these countries' air bases in various parts of the world. While the act officially ended America's neutrality during World War II, it was considered a life-saving action on the part of the U.S. Government to stopping the military advances of the Axis powers in all of the named countries. The data at this site comprise itemized lists of all the shipments to each country and enable history students to conceptualize the extent and scope of the act and its historical and economic implications.

Critical Thinking Questions and Activities

1. Click on the "Army Air Forces" link. Note the number of planes that the Great Britain and the USSR received from the Lend-Lease program. What factors may account for the differences in quantity?
2. Many economic historians postulate that the United States emerged from the Great Depression because of its involvement in manufacturing so many implements of war. Employ the totals listed in the following links for various types of equipment as evidence to support this hypothesis: "Ordnance- General," "Ordnance—Motor Transport Vehicles," and "Ordnance—Ammunition & Explosives."
3. The victor in a war can sometimes be foreseen based on which combatant side can produce or obtain more military equipment to wage it. Visit the *Comparison of Military Production Expenditures* site at http://ww2total.com/WW2/History/Production/military-expenditures. htm. Employ these data and the totals produced in the Lend-Lease program to hypothesize that one cause of the Axis powers' defeat may have been because they were militarily out-produced.
4. After World War II, the United States engaged in a "Cold War" with the USSR. Employ the Lend-Lease data in various categories to show how the United States helped the USSR win World War II. Explain why it was a military necessity to lend the USSR all of this military equipment.

Related Internet Sites

Chapter IX Lend-Lease
http://ww2total.com/WW2/History/Production/military-expenditures.htm

Provides an overview of the Lend-Lease program from the British point of view, together with embedded data concerning the amount of equipment delivered and cost.

Lend-Lease to the Soviet Union
http://lend-lease.airforce.ru/english/documents/index.htm
Click on the "Documents" link to retrieve an itemized list of equipment loaned to the USSR as part of the Lend-Lease program. This site is useful for answering question 4.

LESSONS LEARNED FROM U.S. HUMANITARIAN INTERVENTION ABROAD

URL Address: http://www.gwu.edu/~nsarchiv/NSAEBB/ NSAEBB30/index.html
Site Summary: Since 1990, the United States has been confronted by many humanitarian crises throughout the world that have significant diplomatic, economic, military, and historic implications. In many cases, these crises have a direct cause and effect on American foreign policy. This eighty-six-page report, written by the Department of State's Policy Planning Director Morton Halperin in 2000, provides quantitative data and analysis about U.S. interventions concerning Kosovo (in the former Yugoslavia), Hurricane Mitch (Nicaragua), the Sudan, and Afghanistan. The report also recommends enhanced leadership and coordination, especially when humanitarian crises are in need of military interventions as witnessed with Rwanda and Timor.

Critical Thinking Questions and Activities

1. Under the heading "Annexes (Index)," scroll to "Annex 9, Table 13 Resources for USG Humanitarian Assistance." Study the amount allotted for humanitarian assistance for 1999 to 2001. Research the amounts that other countries spend on humanitarian assistance. Estimate how long the United States will be able to render this amount of humanitarian assistance given its current level of debt. What are the diplomatic and foreign policy implications of not supplying humanitarian aid to other nations during a crisis?

2. Under the heading "Annexes (Indexes)," scroll to the "Afghanistan Case Study." Extract the embedded data concerning the cost of humanitarian aid by various U.S. departments and agencies since 1995. Research and find an update of the allotted amount to the current year. Imagine that you are a U.S. senator on the Budget Committee that oversees and recommends funds for humanitarian aid. Based on past events involving the United States and Afghanistan, what would you

do regarding continuation of humanitarian aid to Afghanistan? Discuss the military, diplomatic, and economic implications of your decision.

3. Under the heading "Annexes (Indexes)," scroll to "Annex 2, Hurricane Mitch Case Study." Extract the embedded data concerning the amount of funds devoted to humanitarian relief for Nicaragua and Honduras. Assume that are the U.S. Ambassador to Nicaragua. What arguments would you make to obtain this level of funding for Nicaragua and Honduras and why?

4. Under the heading "Annexes (Indexes)," scroll to "Annex 3, Sudan Case Study." Extract the embedded data concerning the amount of funds that has been spent on the Sudanese humanitarian crisis. In the case study, there is a reference to "different camps within the administration and on Capitol Hill" about how to help solve the crisis. Imagine that you represent President George W. Bush's administration. Write a persuasive speech, using the data, arguing that the United States must continue humanitarian aid to Sudan to continue to try and stabilize that part of Africa.

Related Internet Sites

Country Studies
http://lcweb2.loc.gov/frd/cs/
Use the drop-down menu to select the respective countries discussed in each relevant case study. The reports contain useful economic and population data plus background and historical information.

Global Humanitarian Assistance
http://www.globalhumanitarianassistance.org/countryprofile/united-states
Provides current data about the amount of humanitarian aid given by the United States and other countries and which countries are the primary recipients. This site is useful for answering question 1.

THE MARSHALL PLAN

URL Address: http://www.marshallfoundation.org/library/index_documents.html
Site Summary: The Marshall Plan or European Recovery Act of 1948 was the brainchild of Secretary of State George Marshall and Department of State Director of Policy Planning George F. Kennan. Essentially, it was a huge humanitarian and economic aid package designed to help European countries recover economically and to stave off the advancement of the Soviet Union. Financially speaking, it was an expansive plan totaling more than

13.3 billion dollars over a period of four years. The Soviet Union was invited to join, but the capitalistic nature of the program and the decision to rebuild Germany was not to their liking.

Their withdrawal included the other member Soviet Socialist Republic countries, thus setting the stage for a future cold war between the United States and other National Alliance Treaty Organization countries. The Marshall Plan documents at this site feature quantitative data in the form of tables and statistics that provide history students with information about its scope and an understanding of its historical significance in aiding a severely damaged postwar Europe and arresting the spread of communism.

Critical Thinking Questions and Activities

1. Scroll to the heading "Marshall Plan Funding Statistics," and click on the link "Marshall Plan Payments in Millions to European Cooperation Countries." Study the pie chart titled "Western Europe's Recovery." Notice that the United Kingdom, France, and Italy received the most funds. Research the threat of communism to these countries from 1948 to 1952. Discuss whether the decision to fund these countries at such a high level was based upon their war damages, potential to elect a communist-dominated government, or a combination of both factors.

2. Scroll to the heading "Committee Reports," and click on "European Recovery and American Aid." Go to pages C5a and C5b of the report and study the tables titled "Balance of Payments Summary for the Sixteen Participating Countries and Western Europe." Employ the data to show how the balance of payments between the United States and the sixteen participating countries was designed to shift the financial burden from the United States to the participating countries from 1948 to 1951. Assume that you are one of President Truman's advisors who has been asked to justify these payments before Congress. What basis do you have for your belief in an eventual payment shift?

3. Read pages E1 to E10 of the report under the heading "Food and Agriculture." Study the tabulated data on page E5 concerning "Production of basic foodstuffs" and on page E7 regarding "Livestock numbers." Explain what the numbers reveal about Europe's food situation for the years 1946 and 1947. Do you think that the committee's estimate of production for the following years is realistic or overly optimistic? Provide an explanation.

4. Scroll to page M4 and read the section titled "Methods of Financing American Aid." Study the table on page M4a titled "Potential Gross Supply of Dollars under Existing Loan and Gift Programs." Assume that you are a member of the U.S. Department of State who has been asked to testify before Congress about the strategic and political bene-

fits of the Marshall Plan. Employ the tabulated data on page M4a as part of your presentation to demonstrate how these costs might pay off in long-term future alliances and mutual aid in future global conflicts.

Related Internet Sites

The Marshall Plan: A Fifty-Year Perspective
http://marshallfoundation.org/library/documents/The_Marshall_Plan_A_Fifty_Year_Perspective_000.pdf
This article is useful for responding to question 4 and also provides a retrospective account of the success of the Marshall Plan in stabilizing parts of western and central Europe.
The Marshall Plan after Twenty Years
http://www.trumanlibrary.org/oralhist/katzmimage1.htm
Furnishes an article assessing the Marshall Plan's effectiveness during the height of the Cold War.

NATIONAL COMMISSION ON TERRORIST ATTACKS UPON THE UNITED STATES

URL Address: http://govinfo.library.unt.edu/911/report/911Report_Exec.htm
Site Summary: On the morning of September 11, 2001, a commercial airliner containing ten thousand gallons of highly flammable jet fuel slammed into the World Trade Center's North Tower in New York City. Approximately seventeen minutes later, a second airliner struck the South Tower. Thirty-four minutes after the World Trade Centers were attacked, an airliner hit the western side of the Pentagon in Washington, DC. A fourth airliner, bound for the U.S. Capitol, was forcibly crashed by heroic passengers in Pennsylvania. The attacks were perpetrated by a group of highly trained terrorists who were members of a group called al Qaeda, which was headed by a Saudi national named Osama bin Laden. In all, 2,981 people lost their lives. The 9/11 Commission Report does not contain traditionally displayed quantitative data. It does, however, provide the most accurate chronology of events leading up to the attack and a minute-by-minute account of how rescuers and civilians coped with the worst terrorist attack in U.S. history.

Critical Thinking Questions and Activities

1. Click on the heading "Report," and click on the "Executive Summary" link. Scroll to page 2 of the report and read the section titled "A

Shock, not a Surprise." The report supplies a chronology of previous terrorist attacks against the U.S. military or civilians from 1993 to 2001. Create a chronological graphic display of these attacks during this period, including the numbers of those killed. Employ the chronology to discuss whether America should have been more prepared for further attacks and/or larger attacks.

2. Scroll to "Section 5 Al Qaeda Aims at the American Homeland" and go to page 5.4 of the report titled "A Money Trail?" Extract the embedded financial data from this section of the report and display it in tabulated form. Describe the main financial data that Al Qaeda, including Osama bin Laden, was being funded up until the 9/11 attacks. Describe how American intelligence agencies might have disrupted Al Qaeda's funding. Which part of the Al Qaeda funds transfers system would be the most difficult to disrupt and why?

3. Click on "section 4" of the report titled "Responses to Al Qaeda's Initial Assaults" and read the part titled "Early Efforts against bin Laden." Make notes on the dates when bin Laden was associated with either attempted or actual terrorist attacks. Assemble the evidence that you have from this section. Do you see any patterns of escalation? Based upon the chronology that you have created, would you have recommended a secret plan to kill Osama bin Laden prior to 9/11?

4. Click on the section of the report titled "Heroism and Honor." The report cites that twelve minutes elapsed after the World Trade Center's North Tower was hit and before the order was given to evacuate the South Tower. Read the report and note the events that occurred during those twelve minutes. Place them in a chronology table. Do you see any critical times or junctures when something else should or could have been done to avoid the loss of life from the attack on the South Tower.

Related Internet Sites

American Jihadist Terrorism: Combating a Complex Threat
http://digital.library.unt.edu/ark:/67531/metadc83950/?q=terrorism
Prepared by the Congressional Research Service, this report contains data about the number of homegrown terrorist attempts and attacks since 9/11.
September 11, 2001
http://memory.loc.gov/ammem/collections/911_archive/
The Library of Congress is maintaining an oral history site about 9/11. It features a list of interviews with people almost immediately after the event and several months later.

NATIVE AMERICAN DOCUMENTS PROJECT

URL Address: http://public.csusm.edu/nadp/
Site Summary: Beginning in 1887, the U.S. Congress enacted several pieces of legislation designed to domesticate Native Americans by dividing up their reservations into allotments that members of each tribe could own separately. This site supplies outstanding quantitative data showing how the passage of the 1887 Dawes Act allowed the government to create allotments within reservations and how the Amendment to the Dawes Act permitted the government to carve out even smaller allotments.

It also provides information about the Act for the Relief of Mission Indians, which deprived southern Californian Indians of their water rights; The Burke Act of 1906, which ended the twenty-five year trust period for the allotments; and the 1910 Omnibus Act, which addressed problems arising from the allotments. Native American scholars debate whether the government's allotment intentions were based on a sincere desire to assimilate Native Americans into a more progressive culture or just a clever method to take more of their land. The result was that tribal relations were effectively destroyed and 37 percent of tribal lands were lost to settlers between 1887 and 1904.

Critical Thinking Questions and Activities

1. Scroll down to "Allotment Data," and click on the link "results of allotment." Read the article titled "What Were the Results of Allotment?" Click on "Table 5" and note the data. The article explores how these acts helped or hurt Native Americans in social and economic ways. Use the data in "Table 5" to measure and evaluate the impact of the various acts on the amount of lands retained or lost.

2. Scroll down to "Allotment Data," and click on the link "results of allotment." Proponents of the acts believed that allotments would, according to Leonard C. Carlson's book, *Indians, Bureaucrats, and Land: The Dawes Act and the Decline of Indian Farming*, "further the progress of Indian farmers" (Carlson, 1981, p. 79). Click on the link "comparing allotment farming with homesteading." What are your conclusions, based upon the data?

3. After reading the article "What Were the Results of Allotment?," click on "Table 3." One of the purported goals of the acts was to provide Native Americans with tillable lands so that they could make progress as farmers. Click on "Table 3." Based upon the data, what is your opinion of this goal's success rate on behalf of the government?

4. Under the heading "Allotment Tables," click on "Table 7 Indian people farming or raising stock in 1915." Note the data on this page.

Write an editorial to *The New York Times* using the data to argue that the goals of this project were an abject failure with regard to promoting agriculture as an occupation for Native Americans.

Related Internet Sites

Native American History Primary Documents
http://cehs.unl.edu/ushistory/online/native/primary.html
This excellent mega-site from the University of Nebraska contains scholarly Internet sites with treaty information and other forms of quantitative data about various tribes and legal matters.
Teaching with Documents: Maps of Indian Territory, the Dawes Act, and Will Rogers' Enrollment Case File
http://www.archives.gov/digital_classroom/lessons/federal_indian_policy/federal_indian_policy.html
Contains lesson plans to accompany primary source documents about the Dawes Act and information about Indian Territory and subsequent reservations.

1929 STOCK MARKET CRASH

URL Address: http://eh.net/encyclopedia/article/bierman.crash
Site Summary: Historians refer to Tuesday, October 29, 1929, as "Black Tuesday" in memory of the day investors in a frenzied panic traded 16,410,030 shares on the New York Stock Exchange. The situation became so dire that stock tickers ran late because the machines could not tolerate the sheer trading volume. As billions of dollars and thousands of fortunes were lost, some investors jumped to their deaths rather than face their utter financial ruin. Much of the stock market data at this Economic History Association site is embedded. Written by Economic History Professor, Harold Bierman, Jr. of Cornell University, it offers a multifaceted perspective on the cause and effect of this devastating economic event that helped usher in the Great Depression.

Critical Thinking Questions and Activities

1. Scroll to "Table 1" showing the "Dow–Jones Industrials Index Average of Lows and Highs for the Year." Note the averages for the years 1930, 1931, and 1932. Why does Professor Bierman term the "crash of 1929" a "misnomer"?
2. One of the causes cited for the 1929 stock market crash was that stocks were overpriced. Refer to the embedded data under the heading

"Were Stocks Obviously Priced in October 1929?" Employ the data to demonstrate why economists are still debating this factor as a probable cause.

3. Scroll to the sections of the article titled "Buying on Margin" and "Investment Trusts." Refer to the embedded data in these two sections and analyze what role they may or may not have played in the stock market crash.

4. Scroll to the sections of the article titled "Investment Trusts" and "The Public Utility Sector." Professor Bierman asserts that "public utility stock prices were in excess of three times their book values." Employ the tabulated data concerning the high and low prices for a 1929 set of public utilities to illustrate how the bursting of the "public utilities bubble" may have been a precipitating factor in the 1929 crash. Click on "Stock Market Crash 1929, 1987, 2000, 2008," a comparative stock market site at: http://www.istockanalyst.com/article/viewarticle/articleid/2688817. Can you find any other types of stocks in these years that were also overvalued? Describe the similarities and dissimilarities among the cited stock market crashes.

Related Internet Sites

Stock Market Crash
http://www.pbs.org/fmc/timeline/estockmktcrash.htm
Part of the PBS History timeline, this site features a generalized, understandable version of the stock market crash that is useful for history and social science students who have not taken any courses in economics.
Stock Market Crash 1929, 1987, 2000, 2008
http://www.istockanalyst.com/article/viewarticle/articleid/2688817
Provides graphs and brief analyses for each of the cited years' stock market crashes.

THE PETER G. PETERSON FOUNDATION

URL Address: http://www.pgpf.org/Issues.aspx
Site Summary: Created in 2008 by former U.S. Secretary of Commerce Secretary Peter G. Peterson, this site is dedicated to building current awareness of the growing financial deficit that the United States has accumulated over the past decades and its consequences for the economic and social well-being of current and future generations. It is replete with quantitative data in the form of charts, statistics, and financial figures. History and social science students will find it exceedingly useful since much of the data goes back to the early nineteenth century. The site also features a solutions section that

students can refer to when researching the implications for some of the posed questions.

Critical Thinking Questions and Activities

1. Under the heading "Fiscal Outlook," click on the link titled "Federal Deficits and Surpluses 1800 to Present." Note the deficits and surpluses on the chart. When have the largest deficits in the U.S. Government occurred? Use this data to write a historical/philosophical essay about the economic dangers of waging war and that war should be the last resort of a country.
2. Under the heading "Fiscal Outlook," click on the link titled "Federal Deficits and Surpluses 1800 to Present." Below this link, click on "More charts," and choose the one titled "Future U.S. debt held by the public is expected to soar to unsustainable levels if current policies remain unchanged." Study the chart data. At what point will the deficit become an untenable percentage of the U.S. gross domestic product (GDP)? Describe the economic, employment, and social effects that a deficit beyond 100 percent of GDP will have on every U.S. citizen.
3. Return to the list of charts and select "The Aging of the U.S. Population." Study the data displayed on the chart titled "The Population of the United States Is Aging Rapidly." Why are the upward trajectories of an aging population so alarming? Describe how an aging population will impact America's healthcare and social services systems? What are your recommendations for solving this future problem?
4. Return to the list of charts and select "Foreign Holders of Public Debt." Study the pie charts for the years 1970, 1990, and 2011. Research which countries are the major holders of the U.S. debt? Discuss the potential economic, military, and political problems of the U.S. public debt versus its holding countries.

Related Internet Sites

Charting the American Debt Crisis
   http://www.nytimes.com/interactive/2011/07/28/us/charting-the-american-debt-crisis.html
   The New York Times has organized an outstanding data-laden site that's filled with the implications and extrapolated projections for U.S. debt problems. It also contains a list of the leading creditors or holders of the debt for assistance in answering question 4.
U.S. Debt Clock
   http://www.usdebtclock.org/

Arranged like a stock ticker tape function, this site provides constant calculations of the U.S. debt.

REPORT OF THE CHICAGO RELIEF AND AID SOCIETY

URL Address: http://quod.lib.umich.edu/g/genpub/aaz9846.0001.001
Site Summary: The city of Chicago was never the same after October 8, 1871, when a ferocious fire began in the west division of the city and spread to the south division, igniting the gasworks. It then spread to the north division and consumed the waterworks, destroying the pumps needed to extinguish the fire. The fire cost three hundred people their lives, destroyed the homes of ninety thousand residents, decimated eighteen thousand buildings, and caused two hundred million dollars in damages. This relief report contains tabulated data about the number and types of building and homes lost; the numbers of people receiving aid in the form of food, clothing, and shelter; and the organizational capability of a city government as it attempted to respond to a great humanitarian crisis.

Critical Thinking Questions and Activities

1. Click page four of the report. Employ the population figures displayed on page four to show how Chicago was a booming city in the years right before the fire. Describe how the explosive population growth drove a need for housing and new buildings. Analyze how the building boom caused government officials to ignore fire safety building and housing codes. How may the lack of fire-safe construction resulted in additional devastation?
2. Click on pages nine to eleven of the report. Create a table using the embedded data to show how many buildings and houses were destroyed by the fire in each division of the city. Imagine that you are an urban planner who realizes that Chicago should view the fire as an opportunity to improve their building structures and placement. Draft a rebuilding plan for Mayor Mason that gives him advice about future building construction (e.g., stone rather than wood), building placement, street widths, and so forth so that he can request city and state funding assistance.
3. Click on pages 145 to 151 of the report. From your analysis of the data, what do you think of the relief efforts? Employ the data to discuss whether Chicago government officials seemed organized and on top of the crisis. Compare the responses indicated in this report to the relief reports about Hurricane Katrina that struck New Orleans on August 23, 2005.

4. Click on pages 222 to 229, "Table of the Diseases and Mortality." The report shows treatment and deaths from a variety of ailments for a year after the fire. Analyze the data for the first three months after the fire. What diseases seem to be causing the most deaths? What conditions may account for these deaths? What could or should Chicago have done to alleviate people suffering from these diseases after the fire?

Related Internet Sites

1871: The Great Chicago Fire
http://www.chipublib.org/cplbooksmovies/cplarchive/chidisasters/greatfire.php
Gives a panoramic view of the aftermath of the fire in many of the city's divisions plus a timeline of events involving the fire.
The Great Chicago Fire and the Web of Memory
http://greatchicagofire.org/
This superb site presents primary sources in the form of eyewitness accounts, period magazine articles, illustrations and images, and artifacts that survived the fire. Quantitative data are included in many of the articles and related links.

THE SALEM WITCHCRAFT SITE

URL Address: http://www.tulane.edu/~salem/
Site Summary: Witchcraft is thought of as the use of supernatural powers to harm or protect people or their property. It has always been a fascinating aspect of history whether it involved the Salem Witch Trials or the concept of scapegoating someone by a charge of witchcraft. This site from Tulane University provides sixteen data sets that open using Excel. They shed light on a time of hysteria from February 1692 until May 1693 that caused nineteen people to be executed, hundreds to be imprisoned, and similar numbers to be accused.

Critical Thinking Questions and Activities

1. Click on the heading "Chronology" followed by the link "Site Map." Click on "Accused Witches Data Set." Employ the data presented to construct a pie chart based on the accused's gender. What percentage of accused witches were female versus male? Why do you think that women were thought to be witches more often than men were?
2. Click on the heading "Chronology" followed by the link "Site Map." Under the heading "Part Two: Chronology," click on the link "Histo-

grams." View the histogram titled "Accusation Histogram Discussion" as one would that of an epidemic. Explain why there were peaks and valleys in the accusation rate. Discuss what factors may account for the pattern of accusation unevenness in the histogram.

3. Click on the heading "Chronology" followed by the link "Site Map." Under the heading "Part Two: Chronology," click on the link titled "Execution Histogram." Why did the executions drop off precipitously by the end of September 1693? Discuss the factors that may have accounted for the cessation in executions and their implications for subsequent outbreaks in surrounding towns.

4. Click on the heading "Chronology" followed by the link "Site Map." Under the heading "Part Two: Chronology," click on the "Andover histogram link." Andover had more accusations than did Salem Village and Salem Town combined. It was the epicenter for the second wave of witchcraft trials. Research what factors may have accounted for Andover being the center for a second major outbreak.

Related Internet Sites

Salem Witch Trials Documentary Archives and Transcription Project
http://etext.virginia.edu/salem/witchcraft/
Sponsored by the University of Virginia, this site features court records, transcripts, and embedded data about the number of victims. It also contains additional information about the outbreak of witchcraft accusations in Andover.

Salem Witchcraft Trials 1692
http://law2.umkc.edu/faculty/projects/ftrials/salem/SALEM.HTM
This site, part of the Famous Trial series from University of Missouri, provides primary sources in the form of trial records, testimonies, maps, chronologies, letters, and biographies. It contains useful information for questions that ask students to draw conclusions about the event.

SAN FRANCISCO GREAT EARTHQUAKE AND THE FIRE OF 1906

URL Address: http://americahurrah.com/SanFrancisco/Municipal Reports/1906/History.htm
Site Summary: At 5:12 a.m., April 18, 1906, San Francisco was struck by the most disastrous earthquake in the history of North America. Although the seismographic rating ranged from 7.7 to 8.25, which is not that high on the Richter scale, the epicenter was only two miles from the city center. While the earthquake caused comparatively little damage, broken water mains left the city virtually defenseless against the subsequent fires. This site contains a wealth of historical data in the form of enumerated reports indicat-

ing the extent of the damage to schools, libraries, police and fire departments, and other public buildings. Click on the link "Index to Earthquake Reports" to access damage reports for various departments.

Critical Thinking Questions and Activities

1. Click on the link "What San Francisco Looked Like the Day Before." Find the location of each of the structures shown on a pre-1906 earthquake map of San Francisco. What circumstances may account for some of them withstanding the earthquake while others were destroyed?

2. Click on the link "What San Francisco Looked Like the Day Before." Under the heading "Department Reports," click on each department and record the financial loss estimates and the number of buildings reported "totally destroyed." Create a bar graph that depicts each department's losses. Employ the graph to assist city officials in establishing priorities for rebuilding the city. Create a set of short- and long-term recommendations for restoring public services based upon your extracted report data.

3. Click on "Official History of the Earthquake and Fire." Create a color-coded map showing areas of the city that were least to most damaged by the fires. What criteria would you recommend that city officials follow for rebuilding? Would you recommend that areas containing the most people or sections of the city that were designated for the conduct of business be rebuilt first?

4. Click on "Official History of the Earthquake and Fire." Much of the damage during the 1906 earthquake occurred in human-created landfill areas. These areas became unstable during the earthquake, causing the collapse of many buildings. Compare the landfill areas described in this report to current ones in San Francisco. What is your opinion of them withstanding a major earthquake today?

Related Internet Sites

The Great 1906 Earthquake and Fire
http://www.sfmuseum.org/1906/06.html
Provides numerous additional reports, newspaper clippings, a map of the earthquake center, and a chronology of events.
Virtual Museum of the City of San Francisco
http://www.sfmuseum.org/loc/movie.html
Presents several brief films from the Library of Congress showing people evacuating the city and camping outside.

THE SOUTHERN DIASPORA AND THE URBAN DISPOSSESSED: DEMONSTRATING THE CENSUS PUBLIC USE MICRODATA SAMPLES

URL Address: http://faculty.washington.edu/gregoryj/dispossessed.pdf

Site Summary: Most history and social science students believe that the "Great Migration," or diaspora from agrarian jobs in the South to factory employment in midwestern and northern states, only affected African-Americans. This site provides a statistically laden article by historian James Gregory that uses census data to show that poor white southerners migrated at even greater rates than did African-Americans. Professor Gregory groups the states that experienced the greatest migration during 1910 to 1970 into a region termed the "Great Lakes States." They include Ohio, Indiana, Illinois, Michigan, and Wisconsin. History and social science students can use the same census tables to study this population change from different perspectives.

Critical Thinking Questions and Activities

1. Scroll to page 112 of the article and view "Table 1." It shows the greatest population increase for Southern-born whites living elsewhere in the United States occurring during the 1950 and 1960 censuses, respectively. What historical and economic events were affecting Southern-born whites during this time period? Were they similar to the ones that Southern-born blacks were experiencing? Create a timeline of these events and juxtapose it against the population increases for Southern-born whites living elsewhere in the United States.

2. Scroll to page 118 of the article and view "Table 2." It shows the 1970 census results for the geographical distribution of former Southerners living in Great Lakes states and California. Note the percentage of former Southern whites living in the Great Lakes states. Hypothesize what their voting patterns might be on social issues such as civil rights, women's right to choose, and gay marriage. Research how Ohio and Indiana voted on these social issues within the past twenty years. Use the data to support your conclusions.

3. Scroll to page 119 of the article and view "Table 3." It shows the average household income and poverty status of both races for the Great Lakes states and California. Which groups of people have suffered poverty in these regions of the country? What factors probably account for the disparity of household income among Southern whites and blacks and Hispanics?

4. Scroll to pages 122 and 125 of the article and view "Table 7" and "Table 9." Compare the educational characteristics of Southern-born

whites and blacks. Are their educational characteristics similar or dissimilar? How does this data either correlate or not correlate with the differences between Southern-born whites and blacks in the occupations of individuals in the civilian labor force. Discuss what you think accounts for this discrepancy between the two groups.

Related Internet Sites

The African-American Migration Experience
http://www.inmotionaame.org/home.cfm?bhcp=1
Sponsored by the Schomburg Center for Research in Black Culture, this site features a timeline, images, maps, and articles about not only the "Great Migration" from 1910 to 1920 but also several others including the recent one back to the Sun Belt states.

Great Migrations Resources Pages
http://www.uic.edu/educ/bctpi/pt3/greatmigration.html
Features an outstanding compilation of links to educational and government sites with information concerning the Great Migration. Many of the sites contain embedded data and statistics that will be useful for research assignments.

STATISTICAL INFORMATION ABOUT FATAL CASUALTIES OF THE VIETNAM WAR

URL Address: http://www.archives.gov/research/military/vietnam-war/casualty-statistics.html
Site Summary: The Vietnam conflict was an undeclared war that began in 1955 between North Vietnam and South Vietnam, which was supported by the United States and its allies. It ended in 1975 with a total communist takeover of Vietnam and withdrawal of U.S. troops. It cost the lives of 58,200 U.S. servicemen and between one million and three million Vietnamese soldiers and civilians. Opposition to the war in the United States began in the 1960s and escalated in 1969 when President Nixon instituted a draft lottery selective service system that essentially abolished the 2-S deferment for men born from 1944 to 1950. Until that time, the war had been waged by a volunteer army that consisted mainly of Americans who were unable to obtain a 2-S deferment because they were either economically or academically unable to remain in college.

This site provides the U.S. casualties list from the National Archives. It presents categorized data that gives students insight about the Americans who died in this undeclared war.

Critical Thinking Questions and Activities

1. Under "Electronic Records Reference Report," click on "Race OMB Name (Race)." Calculate the percentage of "Blacks or African-Americans" who died in Vietnam. Research what percentage of the total population was represented by African-American males in the 1960s and 1970s. Did a greater proportion of African-Americans die in Vietnam than were represented in the total population? Discuss the possible economic, educational, and employment reasons for this statistic.

2. Scroll down to "Vietnam Conflict Extract File Record Counts by Casualty Category (as of April 29, 2008)." Calculate what percentage of the casualties died from "Self-Inflicted wounds." Compare this number with those reported in Iraq for an equal number of service persons. What factors may account for the larger number of self-inflicted deaths in Iraq compared to Vietnam? Refer to the site "US and Coalition Casualties in Iraq and Afghanistan cited under Related Internet Sites" for assistance in answering this question.

3. Scroll down to "DCAS Vietnam Conflict Extract File Record Counts by Incident or Death Date (Year) (as of April 29, 2008)." Note which years had the highest recorded deaths. Research the level of anti-war protests during these years. Analyze what effect these protests may have had on de-escalating the war. Create a histogram that shows the number of protests and the casualty rates for each year of the war as part of the analysis.

4. Scroll to "Vietnam Conflict Extract File Record Counts by Casualty Country/Over Water Code (Country of Casualty) (as of April 29, 2008)." Although the table shows that the majority of U.S. casualties occurred in South and North Vietnam, a significant number of U.S. servicemen died in Cambodia and Laos. Research how the United States became involved with these countries during the conflict and ended up violating the Geneva Accords in March 1969 by secretly bombing Cambodia and Laos in February 1971. Describe the difficulties of containing a conflict or war within specific borders once it starts.

Related Internet Sites

Casualties—US vs NVA/VC
http://www.rjsmith.com/kia_tbl.html
Provides additional casualties data that are specified by battle year, armed forces divisions, and troop levels, etc.

U.S. and Coalition Casualties in Iraq and Afghanistan

**http://costsofwar.org/sites/default/files/articles/10/attachments/
Lutz%20US%20and%20Coalition%20Casualties.pdf**
This paper, written by a Brown university student, contains data about the
number of "self-inflicted" casualties in the Iraq and Afghanistan. It is useful
for answering question 2.

THE 1911 TRIANGLE SHIRTWAIST FACTORY FIRE

URL Address: http://www.ilr.cornell.edu/trianglefire/
Site Summary: On March 25, 1911, New York City experienced the
most lethal industrial calamity in its history. A total of 146 factory workers
died from burns, smoke inhalation, or jumping to their deaths to escape a fire
raging in the shirtwaist factory where they labored. The fire ignited a corresponding storm of outrage as investigators reported locked exit doors, an
absence of fire alarms, accumulated flammable piles of material cuttings,
broken fire escapes, and a lack of fire extinguishers as contributing factors to
such a great loss of life. The New York state legislature responded by passing
a series of occupational health and safety laws making New York a model for
labor reforms in memory of the shirtwaist factory victims.

Critical Thinking Questions and Activities

1. Although the Triangle Shirtwaist Factory was not unionized at the
time of the fire, members of the Ladies' Waist and Dressmakers'
Union Local 25 joined with other charitable organizations to deliver
emergency relief funds to surviving family members. Under "Text
Documents by type," click on the "Report of the Joint Committee."
Scroll through the "Cases Where Relief Was Given." Create tables for
the sixty-four relief cases showing the circumstances for each granted
amount. How and why are there such variations in relief awards? In
your opinion, did the committee distribute the funds equitably?
2. Use the link http://ocp.hul.harvard.edu/ww/nysfic.html to access the
"Fourth Report of the Factory Investigating Commission, 1915, Volume 1." Scroll to "Wages and Wage Legislation" on page thirty-three.
Analyze and tabulate the data on wages paid to girls and women in the
shirt manufacturing industry. Imagine that you are a union organizer
with the Ladies' Waist and Dressmakers' Union. Display and present
the data about their exceedingly low wages in a format that will con-
vince girls and women to join the union.
3. Use the link http://ocp.hul.harvard.edu/ww/nysfic.html to access the
"Fourth Report of the Factory Investigating Commission, 1915, Volume 1." Go to page 199 and view "Table XV Median Rates and

Earnings by Sex and Age." Compare the gender pay rates for each age category. Are women earning less than men? Project the earnings for men and women for fifteen years. Discuss the economic and social extrapolations of your results.

4. Use the link http://ocp.hul.harvard.edu/ww/nysfic.html to access the "Fourth Report of the Factory Investigating Commission, 1915, Volume 1." Go to pages 215 to 216 and study the data presented in "Table XXIV Average Weekly Wage by Time Worked–Up State Shirt Factories" and "Table XXV Annual Earnings–Up-State Shirt Factories." Notice how difficult it was to obtain full-time work in this field and examine the average annual earnings. Research what annual amount you needed to make in the early 1900s to stay out of poverty. At present, the United States ships this type of work to countries such as Vietnam, China, and Cambodia. Research the wages being paid workers for this type of work in these countries. How does it compare to those paid to U.S. workers in the early 1900s? What would be the current annual earnings of textile workers adjusted for inflation?

Related Internet Sites

The Triangle Shirtwaist Fire Trial, 1911
http://law2.umkc.edu/faculty/projects/ftrials/triangle/trianglefire. html
Click on "The Fire Report" to obtain additional quantitative data about the safety deficits and other factors that contributed to the fire.

Women Working, 1800–1930
http://ocp.hul.harvard.edu/ww/topics_work.html
Sponsored by Harvard University, this mega site contains thousands of full-text articles, reports, and quantitative data about the world of work and women in the nineteenth and early twentieth centuries.

TWENTY-FIFTH ANNIVERSARY OF THE 1973 OIL EMBARGO

URL Address: http://www.eia.gov/emeu/25opec/anniversary.html
Site Summary: Although this site, sponsored by the Energy Information Administration, was last updated in 2000, the thirty major energy trends displayed in tables, charts, and PowerPoint presentations provide a quantitative snapshot of how the United States has coped with the shocking effects of a major political and economic crisis that occurred forty years ago. October 1973 was the first time that production and sale of oil was effectively used as a political and economic weapon.

In response to the United States supplying Israel with weapons during the Yom Kippur War, members of the Organization of Arab Petroleum Exporting Counties plus Egypt, Syria, and Tunisia declared an oil embargo. The United States immediately reacted by helping to negotiate a truce among the three countries and experienced a stock market crash. It also realized for the first time that our own supplies of energy were not finite and that dependence upon foreign sources was hazardous for the country's future growth and prosperity.

Critical Thinking Questions and Activities

1. Click on the link "Imported Oil as a Percent of Total U.S. Consumption." Employ the embedded data and chart to explain the economic and political peril that the United States faces by its continued dependence upon foreign sources of oil. The chart ends in 1997. Visit the "Total Energy" site at http://www.eia.gov/emeu/aer/contents.html to update the data through 2012.
2. Click on the link "Percent of OPEC and Persian Gulf World Oil Production." Oil is now in demand by countries such as India and China that previously did not purchase as much. Research these two countries increasing share of a diminishing supply of oil. What is the trajectory for the price of oil in the future? Initiate a class discussion about what may happen if other countries are able to pay higher fuel prices than the United States is able to pay.
3. Click on "U.S. Natural Gas Prices." Use the embedded data and chart to explain the fluctuation in natural gas prices. Research the discovery of vast U.S. shale gas reserves in the northeastern United States and the process of hydraulic fracturing also known as fracking. How might the additional supply of U.S. natural gas reduce U.S. dependence upon imported oil? Do you see fracking as a short- or long-term solution to U.S. energy needs?
4. Click on the link "U.S. Horsepower of a New Vehicle." Employ the embedded data and chart to trace the progress that auto manufacturers have made increasing gas mileage for all types of vehicles from 1997 to 2012 by visiting the following web site at http://www.epa.gov/fueleconomy/regulations.htm. Should the U.S. Government continue to compel American auto manufacturers to produce more energy-efficient vehicles, or should it rely upon the economic laws of the marketplace to improve gas mileage?

Related Internet Sites

Oil's New World Order
http://www.washingtonpost.com/opinions/daniel-yergin-for-the-future-of-oil-look-to-the-americas-not-the-middle-east/2011/10/18/glQAxdDw7L_story.html
Daniel Yergin is a Pulitzer-winning prize author of a book about the history of oil. In this article, he sketches out what the future may be like with diminishing supply and increasing demand.

Total Energy
http://www.eia.gov/totalenergy/data/annual/index.cfm#naturalgas
Contains annual and monthly energy statistics and charts dating back to 1949.

U.S. STRATEGIC BOMBING SURVEY: THE EFFECTS OF THE ATOMIC BOMBINGS OF HIROSHIMA AND NAGASAKI, JUNE 19, 1946

URL Address:
http://www.trumanlibrary.org/whistlestop/study_collections/bomb/large/documents/pdfs/65.pdf
Site Summary: As part of the continuing war with Japan, the United States dropped an atomic bomb on Hiroshima on August 6, 1945, initially killing sixty-six thousand people. Two days later, the United States dropped a second atomic bomb on Nagasaki that killed approximately thirty-nine thousand people. Japan surrendered on August 15, 1945, and World War II ended. This site contains the results of a strategic bombing survey commissioned by President Harry S. Truman to ascertain damage amounts to both cities, the extent of casualties, the response of military and civilian defense, and the impact on Japanese morale. The power of the embedded and tabulated data lies in its immediacy. One can sense that neither the U.S. interrogators nor Japanese responders have fully comprehended what the future terrifying effects of this new military weapon holds for the world.

Critical Thinking Questions and Activities

1. Imagine that you have been asked to prepare a Hiroshima Prefectural Report on the atomic bomb disaster. Extract the embedded data on pages four to ten of the survey report and inform Japanese military and government officials about the devastating effects of the bombing on civilians and property. From what you have read in the report, what would be your recommendations to the Japanese government concerning the possibility of surrendering to the Allied forces?

2. Scroll to pages twenty-three to twenty-five of the survey. Hiroshima and Nagasaki had been relatively untouched from Allied non-atomic bombings during the war. Cite their citizens' responses in a research paper about the Japanese desire to continue the war up until the atomic bombs were dropped.

3. On page twenty-four, U.S. interrogators report that the "certainty of defeat was much more prevalent at Hiroshima ... than at Nagasaki" after the dropping of the bombs. Employ the embedded data about the damages and civilian casualties to explain why the residents of Hiroshima may have experienced a greater sense of defeatism.

4. Read pages twenty-five to twenty-six that discuss people's reaction to the bombings. What percentage of the respondents blamed the United States? Why is this percentage so low? What factors may account for this small percentage of the population that blamed the United States for the devastation wreaked upon Japan?

Related Internet Sites

Hiroshima and Nagasaki Occupation Forces
    **http://www.dtra.mil/documents/ntpr/factsheets/hiroshima_and_
nagasaki_occupation_forces.pdf**
    Provides medical and property damage data about what the U.S. occupation forces observed after arriving in Hiroshima and Nagasaki.
Trinity Atomic Web Site
    http://www.cddc.vt.edu/host/atomic/hiroshim/hiro_med.html
    This site is filled with quantitative data, documents, and photos about the effects of the atomic bombs dropped on Hiroshima and Nagasaki.

THE WEALTHIEST AMERICANS EVER

URL Address:
**http://www.nytimes.com/ref/business/20070715_GILDED_GRAPHIC.
html**
    Site Summary: This site, produced in 2007 by *The New York Times*, measures personal wealth as a percentage of the economy to arrive at a list of the thirty wealthiest Americans ever from 1750 through 2000. The site features a short, biographical sketch of each individual that includes information about how he acquired his wealth. Birth and death dates and the timeline will help history and social sciences students research historical and economic events that may or may not have influenced each cited American's ranking within the thirty. *The Wealthiest Americans Ever* is an example of a histogram that students will not only like to create themselves, but enjoy using for part of their own presentations on this topic.

Critical Thinking Questions and Activities

1. How many of these wealthy men earned their fortunes between 1877 through 1893? This period was also known as "The Gilded Age" or "Age of the Robber Barons." What legal and economic conditions permitted them to amass such wealth? Was there greater or lesser income inequality during this age compared to the present decade?
2. Look up the GDP for 2007. What percentage of the GDP did the men who made their fortunes during the Gilded Age represent? Describe the positive and negative effects that such concentrated wealth has on society and free competition.
3. Of the men whose wealth ranges from $45 billion to $192 billion, how many could be termed monopolists? The Sherman Anti-Trust Act was enacted in 1890 to prevent monopolies similar to those that occurred during "The Gilded Age." Has this act prevented similar monopolistic wealth concentrations in the twenty-first century (i.e., Microsoft, Google, and Facebook)?
4. What percentage of America's wealthiest men gave a substantial portion of their billions to charity or philanthropic causes? Some people maintain that extremely wealthy people should pay a greater percentage of their income in federal taxes. Is it relevant when exploring this issue to consider the total percentage of their annual income that the wealthy expend in charitable contributions—and in tax payments?

Related Internet Sites

The All-Time Richest Americans
   http://www.forbes.com/2007/09/14/richest-americans-alltime-biz_cx_pw_as_0914ialltime_slide.html
Compiled by *Forbes Magazine*, the site producers totaled each individual's wealth in billions at its peak. This amount was compared to the 2006 GDP and converted to dollars to give a contemporary measurement of their wealth.
The 30 Richest Americans of All Time – Inflation Adjusted
   http://www.celebritynetworth.com/articles/entertainment-articles/30-richest-americans-time-inflation-adjusted/
This site is similar to *The New York Times* site, but it is adjusted for inflation and thus reflects contemporary dollar amounts.

YELLOW FEVER EPIDEMIC OF 1793

URL Address: Go to *Google Books* and type in the title *Minutes of the Proceedings the Committee Appointed on Date 14 September to Alleviate the Suffering of the Afflicted*
Site Summary: Yellow fever was a common scourge in American cities during the eighteenth century. A particularly rainy spring created the optimum environmental condition for the *Anopheles* mosquito to breed and bite thousands of unsuspecting Philadelphians, causing a severe outbreak of the fever. It resulted in the death of more than four thousand residents. This site provides quantitative data about the attempt by various government officials and doctors to ascertain the cause of the epidemic, contain it, and care for the ill. Philadelphia was a major U.S. port city in the 1700s, and government officials were challenged to keep the city functioning during such a turbulent time.

Critical Thinking Questions and Activities

1. During the epidemic, a rumor started that African-American people were immune to the fever and therefore could nurse the sick without contracting the disease. A call went out to members of the African-American community to volunteer their nursing services. Go to page 240 of "Minutes of the Proceedings." Compare the death rates between African-Americans and white people. Use the data to support a position either for or against African-Americans nursing fever victims based on their death rates.
2. In the spring of 1793, just before the fever struck, a ship filled with two thousand immigrants from Cap Francais, Saint Dominique, docked. The medical community believed that some of the people on board were carrying the fever. Scroll to pages 240 to 242 of "Minutes of the Proceedings." View the table titled "The Number of Houses, Deaths in the Respective Streets, Alleys and Courts in the City of Philadelphia." Locate an eighteenth century map of Philadelphia. Imagine that you are a medical doctor living during the fever epidemic. Determine if there are a higher number of deaths in streets and alleys nearer to the port. Write a newspaper article describing your findings.
3. As the epidemic spread, thousands fled the city. The mayor advertised in the local papers for volunteers to help. Scroll to pages ten to thirteen of "Minutes of the Proceedings" and scan the list of volunteers. How many people volunteered their services? What groups of people are noticeable for their absence? How would you describe the government response to the epidemic?

4. Scroll to page 201 of "A Statement of the Expenditures of the Members of the Committee Appointed for the Relief of the Sick, etc." Describe the nature of the relief efforts based on the tabulated data. Discuss the extent of relief given by this committee given the circumstances of such a large epidemic.

Related Internet Sites

"A Short Account of the Malignant Fever, Lately Prevalent in Philadelphia"
http://collections.nlm.nih.gov/muradora/objectView.action?pid=nlm:nlmuid-2545038R-bk

Accessible at the National Library of Medicine, this full-text account of the yellow fever epidemic contains data about the number of deaths, types of treatment, and more.

Go to *Google Books* and type in the following title: *An Account of the Bilious Remitting Yellow Fever as it Appeared in the City of Philadelphia in 1793*

Contains some quantitative data regarding the daily weather patterns that were thought to contribute to the spread of yellow fever.

Chapter Five

World History Sites

AFRICAN ACTIVIST ARCHIVE

URL Address: http://africanactivist.msu.edu/
Site Summary: South Africa's history from the period of Dutch and British colonization bears the cultural, economic, and societal scars of slavery, indenture, and unfair laws that culminated in the racist laws of apartheid under the National Government from 1948 to 1993. This site contains thousands of papers, reports, position statements, law, policies, and data that tell the past and recent history of South Africa. The site is searchable from a "Browse" heading under topics such as media type that include video, newsletters, reports, etc. The search engine supports keyword searching under broad topics such as human rights, policing, security, and health.

Critical Thinking Questions and Activities

1. In the search box, type in search phrase "I.B.M. in South Africa." As early as the 1970s, there was a campaign to stop International Business Machines (I.B.M.) Corporation from selling computers and software to South Africa. Click on "View PDF." Extract the monies cited in the report showing the amounts that the South African government paid to I.B.M. to help develop and maintain the apartheid classification system. Display the amounts in tables and employ them to argue that I.B.M. should be banned from conducting business in South Africa because their computers and software systems were helping to create and maintain a police state.
2. In the search box, type in the keywords "human rights violations." Click on the link "Human Rights Violations in Apartheid South Afri-

ca." Extract the statistical data that is presented textually in the article within the following headings: land, removals, pass laws, prison population, and detention. Display the data with graphics in a persuasive manner that will make people in other countries want to support a publicity campaign for South African activists' cause.

3. In the search box, type in the keywords "withdrawal debate." Click on the link "The Withdrawal Debate—U.S. Corporations and South Africa." Extract the data in the text that reveal the extent of the U.S. investments in South Africa. Cite and discuss the data in a research paper to demonstrate the harm they were doing to the non-white South African cause.

4. In the search box, type in the keywords for three different searches: (1) "Remember Sharpeville," (2) "Recent Strikes Involving Over 50,000 Black Workers," and (3) "Soweto 1976—The Struggle against Apartheid." Extract the data from each of these articles. Use the statistics to reveal a pattern of escalation on the part of black South Africans to demand their freedom and civil rights from the current government. After viewing this pattern, why you think that it took until 1993 for black South Africans to abolish apartheid?

Related Internet Sites

The South African Democracy Education Trust
http://www.sadet.co.za/
Contains a three-volume work that provides reports, analysis, and data about how South Africans labored to abolish apartheid and have equal rights under a new South African constitution.

The Truth & Reconciliation Report
http://www.justice.gov.za/trc/report/index.htm
Contains the full text of the six-volume report of the Truth & Reconciliation Commission, which heard testimony about the atrocities committed during apartheid. Although much of the report is textual in nature, there are some bar graphs that graphically depict the damage that apartheid policies inflicted on not only specific individuals but also the entire non-white population.

ARGONAUT CONFERENCE, JANUARY-FEBRUARY 1945: PAPERS AND MINUTES OF MEETINGS

URL Address:
http://cgsc.cdmhost.com/cdm/singleitem/collection/p4013coll8/id/3687/rec/5

Site Summary: The decision about how to reorganize the nations of Europe after World War II ended was made at the Argonaut Conference, also known as the Yalta Conference. President Franklin D. Roosevelt, Prime Minister Winston Churchill, and General Secretary Joseph Stalin met for the purpose of planning what the map of post–World War II Europe would resemble. This site contains not only detailed plans for ending the war but also provides the minutes of the previous major inter-allied war conferences including those of Arcadia (1941), Casablanca (1943), Trident (1943), and Octagon (1944). All of conferences feature quantitative data in the form of troop deployments, battle plans, fuel depots, supplies, and enemy numbers assessments. It is virtually a war-by-the numbers source of primary documents.

Critical Thinking Questions and Activities

1. Sun Zsu's famous book, *The Art of War*, warns against running either ahead of one's supply lines or out of supplies. Scroll to page twenty-two, "Levels of Supply of All Petroleum Production All Theaters." Use these figures to compare and discuss how the Allies were equipped to continue the war versus Germany whose estimates can be viewed on pages twenty-eight to thirty-four.

2. By 1945, the war from Germany's standpoint had become a war of attrition. They lacked sufficient numbers of men who were of military age and fuel to take the battle to the Allies. Scroll to page thirty-six of the report, which gives an estimate of Germany's ground forces for October and January. Despite these figures, it is clear that the Allies were still fighting a dangerous foe. Analyze some of the reasons why Germany was still able to wage war in the face of these statistics.

3. Roosevelt, Churchill, and Stalin also signed an agreement to render supplies to newly liberated countries such as France and Belgium even though the Allies were still waging the war with Germany. Scroll to page forty-nine of the report and note the shipping figures to these countries. Research why France and Belgium were in such need of these supplies. Scroll to pages fifty-three and fifty-five of the report and note the shipping deficits listed. Analyze what the problems were with shipping and how the war continued to affect delivery of supplies. If you were the Supreme Allied Commander of the European Theater of Operations, what would be your priority for the types of essential supplies?

4. While the Argonaut Conference members anticipated the end of the war in Europe, they still needed to wage war against Japan. Scroll to page ninety-nine of the report and study the "U.S. Army Overseas Strengths After V-E Day." Imagine that you are a Japanese spy who

has just discovered these figures. What would you urge your country to do based on the numbers of troops who were going to be re-deployed to the Pacific theater?

Related Internet Sites

Foreign Relations of the United States Diplomatic Papers, The Conferences at Cairo and Tehran, 1943
http://digicoll.library.wisc.edu/cgi-bin/FRUS/FRUS-idx?id=FRUS.
FRUS1943CairoTehran
   Provides the full text of the Tehran and Cairo conferences of 1943, including data concerning troops, supplies, and more.
Military History Online: The Yalta Conference
http://www.militaryhistoryonline.com/wwii/articles/yalta.aspx
   Although no quantitative data exists at this site, history students will find an excellent military analysis of the significance of the Yalta Conference.

THE BERLIN AIRLIFT 1948–1949: FACTS AND FIGURES

URL Address: http://www.nationalcoldwarexhibition.org/learn/berlin-airlift/berlin-airlift-fact-figures.cfm
   Site Summary: In 1946, the population of Berlin, Germany, was 3.2 million people. Divided into four occupied zones and surrounded by the Soviet sector, the city was under joint Allied control until July 1, 1948. On June 24, 1948, the Soviets, in protest over the introduction of the Joint Council's currency reform, began to blockade the land routes into the city from the west. Thus began the largest airlift in history as the western Allies began to fly tons of food, fuel, and other supplies to aid the city's residents. On May 12, 1949, the Soviets lifted the blockade. This site features the "airlift by numbers," and other parts of the site contain excellent background and historical information.

Critical Thinking Questions and Activities

1. The Soviets were counting that the Allies could not maintain the airlift because of the enormous expense. Total the expenses of the Berlin airlift to the United States, Great Britain, and Germany. What was it costing each country per day? Imagine that you are a trusted advisor to Soviet leader Joseph Stalin. Tell him to continue the blockade because the airlift is bound to fail because of economic reasons based on these figures and the related economic and social conditions in the Allied

countries. Why might the people in the Allied countries be unwilling to continue support of the blockade?

2. Great Britain was still under food rationing controls at the time of the blockade. Note the average number of calories per day that Berliners were receiving. Compare it to the number that British citizens were receiving under the food rationing regulations. Imagine that you are a London Member of Parliament. Use Excel or another computer program to create a pie chart showing the disparity. Argue that the airlift should cease at once and that these supplies and funds should go to British citizens who have fought and suffered so much to defeat Germany.

3. Choose what you think are the most important facts and figures at this site to argue that the airlift was really a humanitarian mission and that it would have long-lasting effects with the German people who were re-building their country. Create a table for the data and present the information before a Congressional hearing whose members wish to know the costs of the airlift.

4. In the facts and figures section, note how many people were flown out of Berlin. Click on the "Consequences" link. Note the number of East Berliners who were moving to West Berlin per month. Why were so many East Berliners moving to West Berlin? Compare the standard of living in both parts of the city. If you were an advisor to Joseph Stalin, what would you tell him to try first before building a wall between the two parts of the city?

Related Internet Sites

The Berlin Airlift
http://www.trumanlibrary.org/whistlestop/study_collections/berlin_airlift/large/index.php?action=docs
Contains hundreds of primary, full-text documents in addition to lesson plans and photographs about the Berlin airlift.
The Berlin Airlift
http://www.pbs.org/wgbh/amex/airlift/timeline/timeline2.html
This American Experience site features an annotated timeline with embedded data plus photographs and a teacher's guide.

BOSNIA'S CIVIL WAR ORIGIN AND VIOLENCE DYNAMICS

URL Address:
http://humansecuritygateway.com/documents/WB_BosniasCivilWar_OriginsViolenceDynamics.pdf

Site Summary: In 1991, the republics of Slovenia and Croatia in the country of Yugoslavia seceded and attempted to form their own countries. The Socialist Republic of Bosnia and Herzegovina also seceded, but their attempt at becoming a republic failed because the Bosnian Serbs established their own republic within the area thus initiating a civil war involving atrocious war crimes, the death of more than one hundred thousand former Yugoslavians, and the displacement of 2.2 million people.

This site contains Chapter 7 from a book entitled *Understanding Civil War: Evidence and Analysis Volume 2, Europe, Central Asia and Other Regions* by authors Stathis N. Kalyvas and Nicholas Sambanis. Although its premise is to test a political theory on the cause of civil wars, it is replete with tables and embedded data that history and social sciences students can use to formulate their own interpretations about causes and effects of the Bosnian War.

Critical Thinking Questions and Activities

1. Scroll to "Table 7.1, Income per Capita and Inequality by Region 1988 and 1990," on page 196. Identify which regions had the lowest and highest per capita incomes. What role do you think the lack of economic opportunity and poverty played in starting the Bosnian war?
2. Scroll to "Table 7.3, National Composition of Yugoslavia, 1961-91 by Republics and Provinces, on page 201." The authors use the term "ethnic fragmentation" to describe one of the possible causes of the civil war. Note the top three republics that contain the largest national minority. Compare these republics to the Bosnia Republic. Employ the data to discuss the role that ethnic divisions played in the war.
3. Use the same table to analyze the role that religions divisions played in either fueling or helping to cause the Bosnian civil war. Did the percentage of Muslims increase in Bosnia-Herzegovina from 1961 to 1991? Compare the percentage to that of the Serbs. Discuss this population disparity as one possible cause of the civil war.
4. Many social scientists and historians have noted that discord is less likely in societies that share a common language, religion, and economic level. Refer to "Table 7.3, National Composition of Yugoslavia 1961-91." Identify the former Yugoslavian republics where the people have more in common with regard to ethnicity and religion. Research how these republics have progressed since the break-up of Yugoslavia.

Related Internet Sites

Bosnia in Conflict

http://www.throughmyeyes.org.uk/server/show/nav.23333
Contains background material about the Bosnian Civil War along with
photographs, maps, and testimonies of some of the victims and participants.
**Reports on General International Crimes and Human Rights Violations
in Bosnia and Herzegovina**
**http://www.universaljurisdiction.org/world/bosnia-and-herzegovina-
/565-reports-international-crimes-a-human-rights-violations**
Provides many reports with embedded quantitative data from organizations such as the Human Rights Watch, Amnesty International, and the
World Bank regarding the civil war in Bosnia.

CENSUS OF INDIA REPORTS 1871–1901

URL Address: http://www.chaf.lib.latrobe.edu.au/dcd/census.htm
Site Summary: By 1820, India was part of the British Empire. During
the eighteenth and early nineteenth centuries, Great Britain was in thrall to a
"statistical movement." The data they collected was not, however, simply
reported in traditional tables; it was incorporated into "ethnographic essays"
that contained subjective information about the different Indian populations
under their control. Their purpose in conducting frequent censuses was to try
and coordinate their resources and use them more purposefully for where
they saw the greatest need. For history students, these reports can also be
read and interpreted as British encounters with populations with different
religions, practices, and customs, and how the British attempted to integrate
the Indian populations into their burgeoning empire.

Critical Thinking Questions and Activities

1. Select "Report on the 1871 Census of India" and scroll to page thirteen of the report. Under the report heading "Sex and Age," note the
   ratios of females to males. Scroll through the remaining ratio data and
   population statistics for males and females on pages fourteen to sixteen. What reasons can you find for the population imbalance between
   males and females in certain regions of the country? Research these
   regions of present-day India and find the ratio of males to females.
   Has the ratio changed since 1871? What do you think accounts for
   either the change or lack of change since this time period?
2. Select "Report on the 1871 Census of India" and scroll to page sixteen
   of the report. Under the heading "Religion," note the population statistics for Muslims and Hindus. The British were constantly trying to
   maintain the peace between Muslims and Hindus as populations from
   these two religions clashed frequently over religious customs and

practices. Note the data that appears on pages sixteen and seventeen of the census report.

Create a map showing where the populations of Muslims and Hindus were largest in 1871. Research the Great Partition of India in 1947, when the departing British decided to create the country of Pakistan in an attempt to prevent a civil war between Muslims and Hindus. Explore how the newly created Pakistan reflected the provinces where the majority of Muslims resided in 1871.

3. Select and read the statistics for the "density of population" for each of the 1871, 1881, 1891, and 1901 censuses. Look for increases and decreases in the population data. What areas of India are the most dense in population? What factors may account for such population density? Research current population statistics for the same Indian regions. What have the changes in population density been since the nineteenth century? What problems do you forecast for present-day India based on this population density? Could India have done anything to solve their current problem of population density earlier given the data pattern that existed?

4. Select "Report on the 1871 Census of India" and scroll to the heading "Nationality, language and caste" on page nineteen of the report. Research the data and statistics concerning the population in the various castes on pages nineteen to twenty-four. Refer to the data and explain how the British exploited the caste system as a means of social control while abolishing certain parts of it. Discuss the reasons for their ambivalence to the caste system.

Related Internet Sites

Digital Colonial Documents
  http://www.chaf.lib.latrobe.edu.au/dcd/default.htm
  Funded by the Australian Research Council and hosted by three universities, this site contains travel narratives and additional data and statistics concerning nineteenth century business activities under the British Raj.
Report of the Census of India, 1931
  http://censusindia.gov.in/Census_And_You/old_report/Census_1931n.html
  The data and statistics at this site from the 1880s until 1931 can be used to study change over time and cause and effect regarding demographic issues in India.

THE CHERNOBYL CATASTROPHE – CONSEQUENCES ON HUMAN HEALTH

URL Address: http://www.greenpeace.org/international/en/publications/ reports/chernobylhealthreport/
Site Summary: On April 26, 1986, reactor four at the Chernobyl Atomic Energy Station in Kiev, Ukraine, exploded, releasing two hundred times more radiation than was released from the atomic bombs dropped on Hiroshima and Nagasaki combined. Because of prevailing winds, 25 percent of the land in nearby Belorussia is uninhabitable. Hundreds of children at the epicenter of the blast have been stricken with thyroid cancer.

The cause of the blast was termed "the human factor," or the failure to follow various safety and site maintenance protocols. Although the reports on this web site are maintained by Greenpeace, which has a definite position against nuclear energy because of its potential for permanent damage to the environment and all who inhabit it, the data are presented without editorial comment. Social science and history students may draw their own conclusions.

Critical Thinking Questions and Activities

1. Download the report and scroll to page twenty-one. The Russian government relocated approximately 350,000 people from the most contaminated areas. There are, however, more than five million people currently residing in areas that are still considered contaminated. Employ the data found on pages eleven to fifteen to show how they are at increased risk from many types of cancer. If you were a Russian government official, what steps would you urge the government to take to help reduce the risk of cancer to these people?

2. Download the report and scroll to page twenty-eight, "Cancer in Ukraine, Belarus, and Russia." Because of the prevailing winds, Belarus has experienced more deaths from cancer than other similarly exposed countries. Research what the Russian government has or has not done to compensate people living in this area. Employ the data in this section of the report to argue that the Russian government should assume medical and financial responsibility for Belarus citizens who are diagnosed with cancers usually associated with radiation exposure.

3. Download the report and scroll to pages ten to seventeen. Cite selected data from the "Executive Summary" of the report that can support an argument that current and predicted future cases of cancer are alone sufficient to recommend that nuclear power plants are too vulnerable to future "human error" and that they should be shut down.

4. Download the report and scroll to pages ten to seventeen. Research the statistics of casualties and health effects from the nuclear disaster at the Fukushima Daiichi nuclear plant in Japan in 2011. See the *Fukushima Accident 2011* site under the subsequent section, "Related Internet Sites." Compare the data from the two accidents. What would you recommend to countries that rely on nuclear power based on this data? How would or could you develop a culture of safety?

Related Internet Sites

Chernobyl: The Human Factor
http://www-bcf.usc.edu/~meshkati/causes.html
Provides a list of embedded data concerning the human, environmental, and financial cost of this nuclear disaster.
Fukushima Accident 2011
http://www.world-nuclear.org/info/fukushima_accident_inf129.html
Contains data about the number of casualties and relocated Japanese that resulted from the Fukushima Daiichi nuclear plant disaster in 2011.

THE CHIQUITA PAPERS

URL Address: http://www.gwu.edu/~nsarchive/NSAEBB/NSAEBB340/ index.html
Site Summary: "Follow the money" is a dictum of law enforcement members when trying to uncover fraud and other clandestine activities. In the case of Chiquita Brands International (CBI), the U.S. Justice Department in 2007 discovered that the company had been hiding payments that were disguised through a variety of accounting tricks to Columbian guerrillas, paramilitary forces, military officials, and a government-sponsored Convivir military group in exchange for their conducting business unhindered in Columbia.

The U.S. Department of State designated one of the groups, United Self-Defense Forces of Columbia, which CBI contributed payments to, a terrorist organization. In 2007, CBI agreed to pay twenty-five million dollars in fines for making illegal payments to the United Self-Defense Forces of Columbia. The National Security Archives site contains 5,500 documents that are replete with financial data revealing how the payments were concealed. A selected chronology of memos and transcripts that dates back to 1990 can aid students in an initial exploration of this web of financial deceit.

Critical Thinking Questions and Activities

1. Scroll through the site introduction and click on the link "other accounting tricks." Employ the tables and data in the report to show exactly how CBI concealed the payments from any inquiring U.S. Government agencies. Imagine that you are an attorney with the U.S. Justice Department. Create an indictment of CBI that shows how the company violated the Foreign Corrupt Practices Act.

2. Scroll to "The Chiquita Papers—A Selected Chronology," and click on the link "1997 May 7." Imagine that you are a company executive who has just received a copy of document that you know the Justice Department has in its possession. Use the payments evidence to argue that these figures simply represent the "cost of doing business" in Colombia and that your company's only goal has been to export bananas to the United States and other countries.

3. Scroll to "The Chiquita Papers—A Selected Chronology" and click on various links that reveal the extent of payments to Colombian guerrilla groups and Convivir, the Colombian government-sponsored military group. Imagine that you are a Colombian attorney who is representing several families whose loved ones were killed by these groups. Employ the financial data from these links as evidence for your lawsuit.

4. Scroll to "The Chiquita Papers—A Selected Chronology" and click on various links that contain financial data. Write a newspaper article and use the some of the figures to show that CBI had a mutually beneficial arrangement with the guerrillas, paramilitary organizations, and government-sponsored military groups.

Related Internet Sites

Court Documents Reveal Chiquita Paid for Security
   http://www.ipsnews.net/2011/04/colombia-court-documents-reveal-chiquita-paid-for-security/
Provides a newspaper article that describes the nature of the plea agreement between CBI and the U.S. Justice Department and its future implications.

Underreported: The Chiquita Papers
   http://www.wnyc.org/shows/lopate/2011/apr/14/underreported-chiquita-papers/
This audio clip of the Leonard Lopate Show features an interview with Michael Evans, the chief researcher on Colombia at the National Security Archives. His explanations of the law suit can assist with answers for questions 1 to 4.

COLONIAL REPORTS ANNUAL NO. 1504 GOLD COAST REPORT
FOR 1929 TO 1930

**URL Address: http://libsysdigi.library.illinois.edu/ilharvest/Africana/
Books2011-05/5530214/5530214_1930_1931/5530214_1930_1931_opt.
pdf**

Site Sumamr: After the British subdued the Ashanti and Fante confeder-
acies in a succession of wars in the nineteenth century, they established a
crown colony in West Africa called the Gold Coast. The British district
commissioners administered it through a system known as "indirect rule."
They empowered a permanent group of tribal chiefs in various regions of the
colony to enact and enforce local laws, but through a system of support for
the local chiefs ensured that the policies of Great Britain would always be
paramount.

Despite the use of indirect rule, the Gold Coast made significant gains in
economic and social development. Transportation was much improved with
the building of railroads and an artificial harbor. This site contains a detailed
report that shows the flourishing of a colony under British rule. Its economic
development would lay the groundwork for the colony's future independence
as modern day Ghana in 1957.

Critical Thinking Questions and Activities

1. The British are often criticized for their colonial system, but many
   historians argue that it was beneficial to regions of the world that were
   still developing. Scroll to "Chapter II: Finance" and note the expenditures listed for railroads and postal and telegraph service. Use these
   commitment calculations on the part of British to show a symbiotic
   relationship between the indigenous people of the Gold Coast and the
   British.
2. The British were also instrumental in introducing the cacao tree,
   which eventually became a staple crop and the first that was exported
   from the Gold Coast. Scroll to "Chapter III: Production" and note the
   export tonnage of cacao. Describe the British attempts to stabilize the
   sale of it on behalf of the colony to make it a viable export crop.
3. The global effects of the Great Depression can be ascertained in the
   trade and economic figures in this annual report. Scroll to "Chapter
   IV: Trade and Economics." Note the import and export figures for the
   year in this section of the report. What were people of the Gold Coast
   importing and exporting? How were they affected by the global depression? Compare Ghana's present-day imports and exports. What
   are the similarities and dissimilarities among products? Does Ghana
   seem to be economically affected by the current global recession?

4. Under "Chapter IV: Trade and Economics," scroll to "section 59." Note the export figures for gold. Explain how the British improved mining techniques that resulted in more gold being mined, but also more revenue for the colonial government. Explain how this extraction of the colony's natural wealth probably helped fuel its future independence movement.

Related Internet Sites

A Country Study: Ghana
http://lcweb2.loc.gov/frd/cs/ghtoc.html
Contains historical and contemporary data regarding Ghana's economic and social development that can be used for answering comparative questions.
The Annual Register for 1874: Documents from the Gold Coast during the Ashantee War
Google Books: http://books.google.com
Provides additional background data about the British consolidation of power in the area of West Africa and particularly their subjugation of the Ashantee tribe.

THE DEATH TOLL OF THE RWANDAN GENOCIDE: A DETAILED ANALYSIS FOR GIKONGORO PROVINCE

URL Address: http://www.cairn.info/revue-population-english-2005-4-page-331.htm
Site Summary: In 1994, Rwanda experienced one of the worst genocides in the twentieth century when more than five hundred thousand Tutsis were killed in approximately one hundred days. For years, Tutsis and Hutus, the rival tribe, had contended for political power and resources engaging in several massacres of each other in Rwanda and neighboring Burundi. On this occasion, however, the genocide was highly organized, sanctioned by officials in the Hutu-led government. Even radio stations and newspapers were used to promote hate speech against the Tutsis. Most of the post-genocide reports reveal a wide range regarding the number of victims. This scholarly site rigorously relies upon pre- and post-census data to extrapolate the death toll from one province to show that the death toll was even higher than cited in most reports.

Critical Thinking Questions and Activities

1. Scroll to "Table 1 Distribution of the Population of Rwanda by Prefecture and Ethnic Group in 1991." Study the ratio of Hutus to Tutsis in the 1991 census data. Based upon the comparative population numbers, which prefectures or provinces would probably be the most life-threatening in 1994 if you were a Tutsi? Create a graph showing the most dangerous prefectures for Tutsis. Describe how you might have tried to live in these prefectures if you were a Tutsi in a Hutu-dominated government.

2. The genocide of Tutsis was much worse where Hutus encouraged them to go to assigned places of safety such as Kibeho and Kaduha. Employ the census data in the report to prove that this was indeed the case.

3. Scroll to the heading "Relationship between the Proportion of Tutsi in 1990 and the Annual Population Growth Rate between 1990 and 2002, Estimated for 117 Sectors of Gikongoro." Employ the displayed scattergram to demonstrate how orchestrated the genocide in pre-targeted sectors where there were large numbers of Tutsis.

4. Scroll to the heading "The Relationship between the proportion of Tutsi and the Sex Ratio." In previous massacres between Hutu and Tutsis, women had been spared. Use the census data from Gikongoro province to demonstrate that this was not the case in this genocide and to show how systematic and methodical the Hutus were in executing so many Tutsis. Click on the "Kernel density function of the sex ratio in 2002, for 117 sectors in Gikongoro Prefecture" link for assistance with this question.

Related Internet Sites

Human Rights Watch Reports—Rwanda
http://www.hrw.org/search/apachesolr_search/rwanda
Provides a series of reports containing background and recent material on the genocide in Rwanda.
UN Report of the Independent Inquiry into the Actions of the United Nations during the 1994 Genocide in Rwanda
http://www.un.org/News/dh/latest/rwanda.htm
Furnishes an eighty-four-page report that contains embedded quantitative data about the genocide in Rwanda, including the role of the United Nations in peacekeeping and other functions.

EAST INDIA COMPANY SHIPS

URL Address: http://www.eicships.info/index.html

Site Summary: The East India Company (EIC) was a British megacorporation that enjoyed a monopolistic trade with India, Burma, Malaya, Singapore, and Hong Kong from 1600 to 1874. Its trade consisted of saltpetre, cotton, silk, indigo dye, tea, and opium. The EIC had its own private armies and navies, and functioned as a sovereign government throughout most of the seventeenth and eighteenth centuries, virtually ruling over one-fifth of the world's population.

Governing such an enormous population required that the EIC invest in continuing education and management training for their clerks, seamen, and merchants, thus helping to create the British Civil Service that maintained the British Empire. The company's employees were called "East Indiamen" or "India men." This site provides quantitative information about the EIC's merchant ships from 1600 to 1834, the men who sailed them, and their voyages. The data reveal patterns that aid in understanding the rise, growth, and eventual decline of one of the most highly developed world trading corporations.

Critical Thinking Questions and Activities

1. Click on the "Voyages" link. Under the heading "List of Captured Ships," create a financial historical annual report of the EIC, detailing when more of their ships were in danger from capture by either the French or the Dutch Navies.
2. Click on the "Voyages" link. Under the heading "Wrecked, Missing, and Captured Ships," click on the various alphabetized links. Imagine that you represent the famous insurance company Lloyds of London. Select two decades of "wrecked, missing and captured ships" from the list. Extrapolate from the data you have collected what the chances of a ship going missing, being wrecked, or getting captured would be during this decade. What insurance fees would you have charged the company to insure its ships during this twenty-year period? What other variables would you factor into these two selected decades that might also influence your insurance rate? You may wish to research Britain's wars with France, the Netherlands, and pirates.
3. Select the "Ships" link and click on the various alphabetized links. Note which ships carried guns and during which time periods. Research the historical periods of these time periods and explain why the ships needed to be armed. Research the recent five-year events involving the pirates of Somalia. What defensive measures would you rec-

ommend that ships passing through this area take based on the history of the EIC?

4. Select the "Research" link, and click on "Families in British India Society." Click the link "Fibis database." Under the heading "Heading Military Passages to India," click on the link "List of EIC Recruits to India." Every ship that sailed during the company's history shows the destination. Click on various ships for the time period and employ the data to show how the EIC expanded into various parts of India. If you were the ruler of an Indian state and observing the arrival of new East Indiamen, what steps might you take to prevent the encroachment by this company?

Related Internet Sites

East India Company
http://www.bbc.co.uk/programmes/p0054906
Features the BBC television series about the history of the EIC. Students can obtain background material by listening to and viewing the episodes, and using the archive of articles and timeline of the company's events.

The East India Company
http://www.portcities.org.uk/london/server/show/ConNarrative.136/ chapterId/2764/The-East-India-Company.html
In addition to furnishing a brief history of the EIC, this site contains embedded data about the company's ships, shipbuilding, shipping risks, and the cargoes.

THE FAMINE IN IRELAND: STATISTICS

URL Address:
http://dnausers.dnet.co.uk/dnetnLDQ/famine/birthsat.htm
Site Summary: Between 1845 and 1852, a terrible famine struck Ireland causing disease, starvation, death, and emigration on a massive scale. Approximately two million people either died from the famine or emigrated to countries such as the United States, Australia, and Canada. The cause was a blight that turned the potato, the main source of food for most of the Irish, black, rendering it inedible. Historians study the famine and its effects and legacy by researching the population statistics cited in various Irish censuses performed before and after the famine. The figures reveal how a human tragedy of such significant dimensions can permanently affect the political and social aspects of a country for years.

Critical Thinking Questions and Activities

1. Click on the link "births and the total population." Provide a detailed explanation why there is such a difference in the number of births between the years 1849 and 1850.
2. Click on the "deaths" link. Use the statistics to show that a significant number of deaths during the famine were children. Explain why these numbers were so high for this age group. Research statistics from selected famines in China and Africa. Do you observe any change over time in the data with regard to children's deaths? Imagine that you are an international aid worker assigned to a famine-stricken area of the world. Which age groups do you believe should receive aid first and why?
3. Click on the link "emigration and statistics." Identify which were the peak years for Irish emigration. Research the immigration history of the United States for those years. Can you find any evidence of discrimination and voiced prejudice against the Irish during these years?
4. Select the link "emigration and statistics" and click on the "graph" link. The majority of the emigrants were between the ages of eighteen and thirty-five years old. List some of the reasons why people within these age ranges probably decided to emigrate. Describe what the economic, social, and political effects would be on a country losing so many of its citizens within these age ranges.

Related Internet Sites

The Hunger Years
http://pubs.socialistreviewindex.org.uk/sr189/stack.htm
Contains an overview article with embedded famine data from the periodical *The Socialist Review*.
Sources in the National Archives for Researching the Great Famine
http://www.nationalarchives.ie/topics/famine/famine.html
Furnishes primary sources in the form of embedded census and relief report data about the famine.

GUNS-FOR-SLAVES: THE EIGHTEENTH CENTURY BRITISH SLAVE TRADE IN AFRICA

URL Address: http://www-siepr.stanford.edu/Whatley.pdf
Site Summary: The thought that Africans played an integral part in abetting the international slave trade in the 1700s is hard to accept without the quantitative data to support the statement and an understanding of the cause and effect role of Great Britain, Portugal, Spain, and other colonial

powers. The explosive growth of sugar plantations in British Caribbean and other parts of the Americas in the early 1600s led to a global search for slaves to work the sugar cane fields and an insatiable demand for sugar to enhance seventeenth century diets. The demand for cheap labor to all of these countries from Africa created an insidious trade between the sale of gunpowder and arms in exchange for slaves.

This article, by University of Michigan Professor Warren C. Whatley, cites primary quantitative data to demonstrate the relationship between the slave trade and gunpowder and arms exports. History and social science students need to remember that data were obtained from British historical sources and that data collecting ceased in 1807 when Great Britain officially abolished the importation, sale, and transportation of slaves.

Critical Thinking Questions and Activities

1. Scroll to page 28 and note the graph titled "Figure 4. Transatlantic Slave Trade by National Carrier." Great Britain abolished their slave trade in 1807. Why does the graph show an even greater increase in the number of slaves being exported? Describe what was taking place in economic terms. Research where these slaves were being exported to by the other slave-dealing nations.

2. Scroll to page 29 and note the graph titled "Figure 5. Prices of Enslaved Africans on the West Coast of Africa." Explain why the prices for slaves were rising when Great Britain and the United States had abolished the slave trade.

3. Scroll to page 30 and the note the graph titled "Figure 6. Demand-Side Covariates." Study the graph carefully and note the relationship between the demand for slaves and the price of sugar. Imagine that you are William Wilberforce, the great British abolitionist and Member of Parliament. Employ this data to urge your countrymen to establish a boycott of all sugar consumption similar to the lettuce and grape boycotts led by Caesar Chavez on behalf of the United Farm Workers in the early 1970s.

4. Scroll to page 31 and note the graph titled "Figure 7. Supply-Side Covariates." Discuss the implications of the correlation between military expenditures and gunpowder sales and the number of slave exports. The author of the article asserts that this relationship has caused the contemporary gross domestic products of major slave-exporting African countries and the southern states of America to be significantly lower than their counterparts. Research and confirm his assertion and propose some reasons for this effect.

Related Internet Sites

Internet Sites Relating to Slave Movement during the Eighteenth and Nineteenth Centuries
http://www.disc.wisc.edu/archive/slave/slavelinks.html
Contains a series of related links about the transatlantic slave trade, many of which feature quantitative data.

Slave Movement during the Eighteenth and Nineteenth Centuries
http://www.disc.wisc.edu/archive/slave/index.html
Furnishes quantitative data concerning the number of slave ships and their routes between Africa and the Americas from the eighteenth and nineteenth centuries.

THE HISTORY OF THE PRESENT STATE OF THE OTTOMAN EMPIRE

URL Address: Go to Google Books and type in the above site title.
Site Summary: Sir Paul Rycaut (1629–1700) was not only a British diplomat but also an able historian and a keen observer of other countries' cultures. For five years, he was employed as the Secretary to the Ambassador to Constantinople. In 1665, he presented his sixty-six chapter book, *The History of the Present State of the Ottoman Empire*, to Great Britain's Secretary of State. His writing was deemed so perspicacious that he was appointed the Consul for the Levant Company in Izmir (present day Smyrna), a post that he held for eleven years.

For history students, Sir Paul's book sheds light on the political, military, and religious organizations of the Ottoman Empire during an era of decline. His exact figures about the Ottoman Empire's military and naval strength were revealing sources of information for assessing the stability of an empire and what threat it might pose to the British Empire. A comparable body of primary sources about this period of Ottoman history does not exist.

Critical Thinking Questions and Activities

1. Scroll to "Chapter V," pages fifty-one to fifty-five. Note the numbers of servants and officers serving the sultan's person or court in these pages. What may the numbers be evidence of? Do you see the number of government positions as evidence of the continued wealth of the Ottoman Empire or its possible corruption and decline? Using the data, write a diplomatic cable that carefully argues both positions and allows the British Secretary of State to draw his own conclusions.
2. Scroll to "Chapter XII" and read pages 94 to 105. On page ninety-four, Sir Paul is quoted as saying, "It is impossible to describe the

wealth and ways of gain exercised by these potent governors." Extract the data that is embedded in the descriptions of the wealth of the province governors. Use the data to show how the governors go about enriching themselves at the empire's expense. Write an editorial to the local newspaper using some of the data as evidence of a corrupt government.

3. Scroll to "Chapter XIV" and read pages 112 to 119. When the Turks conquered a country or territory, they exacted tribute in the form of regularly paid money and or agricultural products or goods. Use the tribute data embedded in pages 112 to 119. Choose one of the conquered territories as an example. Write a detailed report to the newly appointed Turkish governor demanding that the tribute be reduced because it is an extreme hardship on the local inhabitants.

4. Read "Chapter III" about the Turkish militia beginning on page 325. Sir Paul writes about an enormous Turkish army and provides data regarding its costs. Every empire must balance the costs of productivity versus security. Note the tables detailing the numbers of militia in various ranks on pages 330 to 340. Employ the data to write an assessment to the sultan warning him that his empire is in danger of future collapse because too much of the Ottoman economy is dedicated to protecting and securing its borders.

Related Internet Sites

Forced Population Transfers in Early Ottoman Imperial Strategy: A Comparative Approach
   http://www.umich.edu/~turkish/ottemp.html
   This senior year thesis by Princeton University graduate Paul Lovell Hooper includes embedded data and a table showing the large numbers of people that the early Ottoman Empire forced to move to different part of their empire as part of their plan to expand and secure even more territory.
The Ottoman Empire: Resources—University of Michigan
   http://www.umich.edu/~turkish/ottemp.html
   Provides a compilation of links including maps and information about the history and culture of the Ottoman Empire that can be used as background information when reading chapters of Sir Paul Rycaut's book.

IRANIAN PRODUCTION OF 19.75 PERCENT ENRICHED URANIUM: BEYOND ITS REALISTIC NEEDS

URL Address:
http://isis-online.org/uploads/isisreports/documents/Twenty_percent_production_15June2012.pdf

Site Summary: Iran is one of the largest countries in the Middle East. Since 1979, it has been an Islamic Republic and does not recognize the state of Israel. Starting in the 1950s, it has had a nuclear power program and ranks seventh in the world's production of uranium hexafluoride. This compound is necessary for the uranium enrichment process that produces fuel not only for nuclear reactors but also nuclear weapons.

Iran has always stated publicly that it is creating nuclear fuel solely to power its nuclear power plant, but many countries, including the United States and Israel, contend that Iran is also producing uranium hexafluoride to create nuclear weapons. This Institute for Science and International Security report provides tabulated data and embedded statistics indicating that Iran is almost at the point of producing sufficient amounts of enriched uranium to create nuclear weapons.

Critical Thinking Questions and Activities

1. Scroll to page ten of the report and study the graph results titled "Figure 1: Average Separative Capacity per Centrifuge in Cascades 1 and 6 at the PFEP and Cascades 1-4 at the FFEP." Explain how increasing the number of centrifuges may enable Iran "to cheat in plain sight" even with the safeguards put in place by the International Atomic Energy Agency. Assume that you are a member of the National Security Council who has just been shown this table and read the report. What would you advise the president of the United States to do at this point?

2. Scroll to page ten of the report and study the graph titled "Figure 2: Cumulative Iranian LEU Distribution." Employ this chart as evidence to argue that Iran is producing far more low-enriched uranium (LEU) than it needs to power its nuclear power plant.

3. Scroll to page twelve of the report and study the graphs titled "Figure 4: Projections for Production of 19.75 Percent LEU Hexafluoride in Iran" and "Figure 5: Cumulative Projections of LEU Hexafluoride Production in Iran." Based on these projections, at what date do you believe Iran will have sufficient LEU to produce a nuclear weapon(s)? Discuss what the implications are for Israel and the United States based on your projections.

4. Scroll through pages ten to twelve of the report. Assume that you are an Iranian government official charged with negotiating with the U.S. Government concerning Iran's nuclear weapons capability. Employ the same data shown in these graphs to deny that Iran is determined to produce nuclear weapons.

Related Internet Sites

AEI Iran Tracker
http://www.irantracker.org/basics
Click on the heading "nuclear" for additional quantitative data about
Iran's nuclear program. This site also contains useful background information.
**Federation of American Scientists FAS Special Report No. 2 October
2011: Towards Enhanced Safeguards for Iran's Nuclear Power Program**
**https://www.fas.org/pubs/_docs/specialre-
port2_iran_nuclear_program.pdf**
Provides a report with some quantitative data about how to prevent Iran
from weaponizing their sources of uranium.

JEWISH EMIGRATION FROM GERMANY 1933 TO 1939

**URL Address: http://www.ushmm.org/wlc/en/article.php?ModuleId=
10005468**
Site Summary: In January 1933, German Jews comprised less than 1
percent of the population. Upon the installation of the Third Reich under
Chancellor Adolf Hitler, they were immediately subject to a graduated series
of anti-Semitic harassment laws and policies that German Jews perceived as
extremely dangerous and life-threatening. Approximately 113,000 eventually
emigrated to other countries. The emigration of German Jews from 1933 to
1939 did not, however, adhere to an ascending linear pattern, despite a similar persecution schema on the part of the Nazi government.

As more anti-Jewish laws, policies, and measures were put into effect,
more German Jews may have desired to emigrate, but they were constricted
by many factors including other countries' quotas and the confiscation of
their personal property and savings by the German government. Most of the
emigration data at the relevant sites are embedded within the text. The numbers and percentages, however, are robust in showing a concerted effort on
the part of the Nazi government to force German Jews onto the eventual path
to concentration camps and death chambers.

Critical Thinking Questions and Activities

1. In the "Holocaust Encyclopedia" search box, type the keywords "emigration map." Extract the data showing how many German Jews emigrated to various countries and create a table displaying the numbers
for each country. What emigration patterns do you observe? Analyze
the reasons for the patterns that you observe.

2. In the "Holocaust Encyclopedia," read the article titled "German Jewish Refugees, 1933-1939." Extract the embedded data about the number of German Jewish refugees from 1933 to 1939 and create a graph. Discuss the probable reasons for the variations in the years that you observe in your graphed results.

3. Use a favorite search engine and type in the keywords "Jewish Emigration from Germany in the First Years of Nazi Rule" (at http://www.zupdom.com/icons-multimedia/ClientsArea/HoH/LIBARC/LIBRARY/Themes/Jews/Niederla.html). Less than 13 percent of German Jews were working in what are considered to be "professions" in 1933 to 1939. Yet 20 percent of them emigrated to other countries. Read the article about this pattern and extract the embedded data. Discuss what factors intrinsic and extrinsic may have accounted for more professionals emigrating than non-professionals.

4. In the "Holocaust Encyclopedia" search box, type the keywords "German Jewish Refugees, 1933-1939." Extract the embedded data showing the variation pattern in emigration during these years. One factor that is put forth as a reason for a slowing of emigration during this period is that Germany seemed to experience some political stability. Research this phenomenon as a contributing factor to the emigration variation pattern.

Related Internet Sites

Emigration and the Evian Conference
http://www.ushmm.org/wlc/en/article.php?ModuleId=10005520
Contains an overview and some embedded data about the unsuccessful conference that President Roosevelt convened in Evian, France, with thirty-two countries in an attempt to establish an international organization to accept more German Jews in each of their respective countries.

Library Themes: Anti-Jewish Policy
http://www.zupdom.com/icons-multimedia/ClientsArea/HoH/LIBARC/LIBRARY/Themes/Policy/Policy.html
Contains a series of scholarly articles with quantitative data about all of the anti-Semitic laws and policies enacted against German Jews beginning in 1933.

LENIN: THE DEVELOPMENT OF CAPITALISM IN RUSSIA

URL Address: http://www.marxists.org/archive/lenin/works/1899/devel/index.htm#Chapter4
Site Summary: Vladimir Ilich Ulyanov, also known as Lenin (1870–1924), was the father of the Russian Revolution and the first Premier

of the Soviet Union from 1922 and 1924. He came from an educated family and passed exams to obtain a law degree. As economic and social conditions deteriorated in Russia with an increasingly repressive monarchy under Tsar Nicholas II (1894–1917), Lenin was drawn to the economic and social ideas proposed by Karl Marx in his groundbreaking book, *Das Kapital*.

Beginning in the 1880s, Lenin began to write pamphlets, articles, and books setting forth his ideas for a new classless form of government that the world would recognize as communism. Although his writings total fifty-four volumes, Chapters 4 and 5 contain embedded and tabulated data from the late 1880s that show the economic success of the Tsar Alexander II's (1855–1881) "Great Reforms" and ironically, Lenin's positive views of capitalism.

Critical Thinking Questions and Activities

1. Select "Chapter IV. The Growth of Commercial Agriculture and click on the link General Data on Agricultural Production in Post-Reform Russia and on The Types of Commercial Agriculture." Study the data in the table titled "Fifty Gubernias of European Russia." Does the data reflect the success of "The Great Reforms" promulgated by Tsar Alexander II? Describe those reforms and their impact on agriculture in Russia. Discuss why it may have been too little, too late.

2. Select "Chapter IV. The Growth of Commercial Agriculture," and click on the link "The Commercial Grain-Farming Area." Note: a chetvert = 5.98 bushels, and a gubernia = an administrative territorial unit that is similar in size to a province. There are three untitled tables showing an increase in grain production as a result of "The Great Reforms." Find grain production statistics post 1917. What change do you see over time? Is Russia still exporting grain after World War I?

3. Select "Chapter IV. The Growth of Commercial Agriculture," and click on the link "III. The Commercial Stock-Farming Area. General Data on the Development of Dairy Farming." Lenin is clearly providing evidence that the injection of capitalism has resulted in a statistically significant increase in stock and dairy farming. Explain what happened to these parts of Russian agriculture after 1917. What factors accounted for these changes during Lenin's term as Premier of Soviet Russia?

4. Select "Chapter V. The First Stages of Capitalism in Industry," and click on the link "The Differentiation of the Small Commodity-Producers. Data on House-To-House Censuses of Handicraftsmen in Moscow Gubernia." The data from the tables and charts is from 1894 and 1895. Compare this data with economic data from the United

States and European countries. Do you think that Russia is on par with these countries or behind?

Related Internet Sites

Lenin Selected Works
http://www.marxists.org/archive/lenin/works/sw/index.htm
Contains three volumes of Lenin's writings within chronological periods. History and social science students will find them helpful in researching Lenin's reasoning on capitalism as a form of government.
Russia: A Country Study
http://countrystudies.us/russia/
Provides historical background and broad economic history data about Russia before and after the Russian Revolution in 1917.

MIGRATION INFORMATION SOURCE–GLOBAL DATA CENTER

URL Address: http://www.migrationinformation.org/GlobalData/
Site Summary: The Greek dramatist Euripides stated that, "there is no greater sorrow than the loss of one's native land." Human migration is defined as movement of an individual or group from one area to another. It has many causes that range from economic, political, philosophical, religious, and social to military. People leave their country to flee war, seek asylum from political prosecution, seek jobs, practice their religion, be free of discrimination, or simply to find sufficient water and food to survive.

Migration can have deleterious effects on the countries and territories that receive them. The numbers of migrants can be overwhelming to a country experiencing similar problems or to a country that is not prepared as a society to accept and assimilate them. The migration data at this site allows students to track, analyze, chart, map, and track trends in human migration from the 1950s to the present day.

Critical Thinking Questions and Activities

1. Click on "Country Resource," and choose "United States." Select "US Historical Trends," and click on the link "Annual Number of New Citizens 1920 to 2010." Note the graph that shows the data from 1910 to 2010. Find a timeline of world events from this time range and impose it in the form of a mash-up (combine data about events from more than one source) on the graph. What events might account for some of the lows and highs in the numbers of immigrant coming to the United States during this time period?

2. Click on "Country Resources," and choose "Japan." Scroll to the article "Japanese Immigration Policy: Responding to Conflicting Pressures." Scroll to "Table 1 Foreign Nationals Registered in Japan." Japan has followed a practice of homogeneity within their borders for hundreds of years. Now, however, they are under intense pressure to admit migrants because of increasing labor shortages in specific fields and an aging population.

   Note which countries the majority of their migrants are coming from during 1995 to 2000. What could be Japan's reasons for accepting foreign nationals from those countries? Discuss the drawbacks and benefits to a homogeneic population. What problems do you predict for Japan in the future given this demographic trend?

3. Click on the "MPI Data Hub" link. Select "Country and Comparative Data." Under the heading "Quick World Migration Stats," choose "Top Ten Countries with the Largest Number International Migrants 2010." Research the possible reasons why these countries continue to receive so many international migrants. Describe the benefits and drawbacks to their indigenous populations.

4. Click on the "MPI Data Hub" link. Select "World Migration Map." Click on each of the "Sending Regions" of the world. Based on the graphs, which region is sending the most migrants? Use the data to analyze the reasons for this diaspora. What would you recommend that this region of the world try to achieve to stop the loss of human capital?

Related Internet Sites

Office for International Statistics UK
   http://www.ons.gov.uk/ons/taxonomy/index.html?nscl=
International+Migration
   Supplies statistics and data concerning the results of Great Britain's most recent census results about international migration.
What is Human Migration? Types of Migration
   http://www.nationalgeographic.com/xpeditions/lessons/09/g68/migrationguidestudent.pdf
   Published by National Geographic, this site contains many additional links to statistical and data-driven sites about human migration.

THE NANKING MASSACRE PROJECT

URL Address: http://www.library.yale.edu/div/Nanking/findingaid.html
   Site Summary: No country in the world has a monopoly on either virtue or vice, and that is certainly true in the case of Japan during World War II.

The Nanking Massacre was one of the hidden holocausts of the war. When the Japanese invaded the ancient Chinese city of Nanking (Nanjing) in December 1937, they systematically set about torturing and murdering three hundred thousand Chinese civilians. This site, sponsored by Yale University, contains archived digital documents and photos of that terrible event that were witnessed by American missionaries living and working in Nanking. While most of the documents are textual in nature, some contain quantitative data about the damages that the battle had on the residents of Nanking. They are especially informative about the extent of the massacre.

Critical Thinking Questions and Activities

1. "Scorched earth policy" is defined as a "military strategy which involves destroying anything that may be useful to the enemy." Scroll down and click on "NMPO249 War Damage in the Nanking Area." Pages seventeen to twenty-three present data about farm losses in the massacre. Employ the data as evidence of a Japanese "scorched earth policy" in Nanking. Explain how this policy created additional pain and suffering for the massacre survivors. Extrapolate how many more became delayed massacre victims because of the loss of food, crops, and seed.

2. Scroll down and click on "NMPO249 War Damage in the Nanking Area." Pages twenty-three and twenty-four contain embedded data under the heading "War and Persons." How does the data provide evidentiary support that there was a massacre of enormous proportions in Nanking? Employ the data to show how this massacre may still haunt Chinese-Japanese relations.

3. Scroll down and click on "NMPO249 War Damage in the Nanking Area." Page thirty-three displays data concerning the gender and age range of the victims. Discuss how this data provide critical evidence of a massacre and how it violated not only the Japanese War Code but also the rules of the International Military Tribunal of the Far East.

4. Scroll down and click on "NMPO249 War Damage in the Nanking Area." Scroll to pages thirty-six to thirty-eight of the report. Study "Tables 10 to 14." Employ the data about "looting and losses of buildings and contents" as supporting evidence of grievous damage to noncombatants. Japan paid out less than 1 percent of the amount that Germany has paid in war reparations to its victims. Imagine that you are a lawyer specializing in international law and war reparations. Employ the data on these pages to argue that survivors of the massacre or their relatives are entitled to compensation by the Japanese government.

Related Internet Sites

The Nanjing Incident Recent Research and Trends
http://www.japanesestudies.org.uk/articles/Askew.html
Provides current analysis of the research into the massacre including information about how the victim data continues to be interpreted and misinterpreted.

War and Reconciliation: A Tale of Two Countries
http://www.japantimes.co.jp/text/fl20080810x1.html
Contains a newspaper article about the extent of Chinese-Japanese reconciliation since the Nanking massacre. This site is useful for responding to question 2.

THE NORMANDY INVASION: D-DAY, 1944

URL Address: http://www.history.army.mil/html/reference/Normandy/normandy.html
Site Summary: As the fog lifted from the Normandy coast on June 6, 1944, German forces found themselves staring at the world's largest armada comprised of more than five thousand ships filled with more than one hundred thousand Canadian, British, and American military men. Although German military leaders anticipated an invasion, the destination and attack date were such a surprise that it helped reduce Allied forces' casualties. D-Day succeeded in liberating most of the French interior by the end of July and initiated the next military operation towards the overall defeat of Nazi Germany.

The casualty data are incomplete for the specific day and differ according to the period of time included in the tabulation. Casualties, however, are still significant, with an estimated 10,000 to 10,500 Allied soldiers and 6,500 German soldiers losing their lives. This site provides an overview of the entire operation along with tables and embedded data concerning the numbers of military personnel, supplies, and weapons needed to launch one of the world's most successful amphibious assaults.

Critical Thinking Questions and Activities

1. Click on the link "Outline of Operation Overlord." Scroll to page three, and study "Table 6 "The Build- Up of U.S. Forces." Calculate the percentage increase in troops from June 6 to October 6, 1944. Explain why the Allies believed that they could increase their forces safely by this percentage ninety days after D-Day. Research the number of German forces that the Germans had in the Normandy area. Do

you think that the D-Day +ninety plans were realistic given the estimates of enemy troops in the area?

2. Click on the link "Outline of Operation Overlord." Extract selected embedded data to demonstrate how meticulously the first phase of D-Day was planned. Research how this systematized approach was transferred to the automobile and aerospace industries in the 1950s. How may this systematic assembly line style of production and distribution that was learned and practiced during World War II have given American industries an economic advantage over our European counterparts?

3. Click on the link "Neptune: Training for the Mounting and Operation, and the Artificial Ports Chapters 1 & 7." Click on the link "Tiger E-boat Attack" in section 256. Planning for the invasion of Normandy involved several major practice assaults, including one titled Operation Tiger. Extract the data indicating that more U.S. soldiers died in this practice assault than died in the first assault of Utah beach. Read the recorded deficiencies after the assault. Discuss what lessons were learned from Operation Tiger that may have saved lives in the Normandy invasion.

4. Click on the heading link "WWII." Scroll and click on the link "The Role of Technical Services in Overlord." Click on link "Chapter VI Preparations for Invasion." Read pages 169 to 200. Write a paper citing much of tabulated and embedded data to demonstrate how the plans for medical services reflected the gargantuan scope and extent of the invasion.

Related Internet Sites

The Battle of Normandy
http://www.dday-overlord.com/eng/index.htm
Contains an overview of the battle plus primary sources with quantitative data about specific operations and planning activities.
D-Day June 6, 1944
http://www.army.mil/d-day/
Scroll to the bottom of the homepage and click on the "Resources" link to obtain a list of additional Normandy invasion Internet sites. Many of them feature quantitative data.

ON THE MODE OF THE COMMUNICATION OF CHOLERA

URL Address: http://www.ph.ucla.edu/epi/snow.html
Site Summary: Cholera still claims the lives of thousands of people per year worldwide. It is caused by drinking or consuming feces in contaminated

food or water. The resulting intestinal upset causes an extreme loss of body fluids that many times results in death from extreme dehydration. In 1854, London experienced an outbreak of cholera. Using statistics and vectoring analysis, Dr. John Snow correctly identified the source of contamination as a well on Broad Street. His brilliant deployment of quantitative data convinced city officials to disable the well's pump handle, which succeeded in stemming the epidemic. This site, from the University of California, Los Angeles, features zoom maps and the data that Dr. Snow used to solve the epidemic.

Critical Thinking Questions and Activities

1. Click on the link "Mapping the 1854 Broad Street Pump Outbreak." Explain how Dr. Snow relied upon maps and the corresponding numbers of deaths to zero in on the epicenter of the outbreak.
2. Click on "Part II" of Dr. Snow's book, *On the Mode of Communication of Cholera.* Click on the link "Table of Attacks and Deaths near Golden Square." What are the reasons for the increase in death rates? Explain how the incidences of illness and deaths were employed by Dr. Snow to confirm an epidemic. Discuss how Dr. Snow's investigative methods laid the foundation for future contemporary epidemiological studies.
3. Click on "Part III" of Dr. Snow's book and link to "Table II." What variable can explain the higher death rates in certain sections of the city? Explain how Dr. Snow reached his conclusions using quantitative data.
4. Click on "Part II" of Dr. Snow's book and refer to "Tables III to XII." Employ the data in these tables to show where the most dangerous areas of the city were for exposure to cholera. Research what classes of people lived in these London areas during this time period. Write an editorial for a liberal newspaper citing Dr. Snow's data to show that the poor were the most likely potential cholera victims.

Related Internet Sites

John Snow and the Cholera Epidemic
http://www.hydroville.org/system/files/u3/John_Snow_2_05.pdf
Employs data and ratios within lesson plans about Dr. John Snow and his cause and effect discovery surrounding the London 1854 cholera epidemic.
Young Epidemiology Scholars Competition
http://yes.collegeboard.org/teaching-units/discipline
Scroll through this interesting site to find social sciences and history teaching units and lesson plans based on actual epidemics throughout history.

PALESTINIAN CENTRAL BUREAU OF STATISTICS

URL Address: http://pcbs.gov.ps/site/507/default.aspx
Site Summary: Despite the 1992 Oslo Accords that promised a future Palestinian state, sovereignty is still a mirage for a group of people who share a common language, religion, and memories of their former homes between the Mediterranean and Jordan River in the current nation of Israel. The Palestine National Authority governs only part of the West Bank located on a ridge of hills between the Mediterranean Sea and Jordan River and the Gaza strip, a narrow piece of land at the southern end of the coastal plain. In 1997, the Palestinian Central Bureau of Statistics undertook a census of the two noted areas for the purposes of voter registration, as well as to highlight the unique problems and challenges faced by the more than 3.9 million people who are officially stateless and totally dependent upon foreign assistance for survival.

Critical Thinking Questions and Activities

1. Select the heading "Statistics." Scroll down and click on the link "Population Projections," then click on "Estimated Population in the Palestinian Territory Mid-Year by Governorate, 1997-2016." Calculate the percentage population increase for the Palestinian Territory, West Bank, and Gaza Strip, respectively, from 1997 to 2016. Convert the statistical results to a bar graph. Compare your findings to population projections for Israel at *Projections of Israel's Population until 2025* at http://www.cbs.gov.il/publications/popul2005/popul2005_e.htm. Discuss what these demographic trends imply for both countries.

2. Select the heading "Statistics." Scroll down to the "Labour Force" heading, and click on the "Unemployment" link. Click on "Unemployment Rate among Labour Force Participants in the Palestinian Territory by Governorate and Sex, 1997-2011." Extract the data for the top ten areas showing the highest unemployment rates within the Palestinian territories for the past five years. Research what the level of violence has been in these areas compared to the top ten areas with the lowest unemployment rates.

3. Citizen security is a quality of life indicator. Select the heading "Statistics." Under the heading "Crime and Victimization," click on "Crime." Under "Main Indicators," click on "Main Indicators Related to Crime and Victimization in the West Bank." What do these indicators suggest about the quality of life for Palestinians living in the West Bank? Research such indicators for other countries. How do those of the Palestinians compare with other countries? What are the implica-

tions of these statistics for civil unrest and terrorist attacks against Israel?

4. Select the heading "Statistics." Scroll to the statistics concerning "Domestic Violence," "Poverty," and "Living Conditions." Compare these statistics to those for Israel. Imagine that you are an Israeli demographer tasked with preparing a report on the future of the Palestinian territories surrounding Israel. Employ the statistics within these categories to forecast what the Palestinian people may do within the next few years if these living conditions persist.

Related Internet Sites

Key Development Forecasts for Palestine
http://www.ifs.du.edu/ifs/frm_CountryProfile.aspx?Country=PS
Developed by International Futures, this site features significant numbers of graphs, statistics, and embedded quantitative data about the population, health, and economy of Palestine.
Palestinian Authority: Other Useful Links
http://www.pcbs.gov.ps/site/632/default.aspx
Contains embedded data within lists, reports, and other links about the economic and social conditions of the Palestinian territories.

PIRACY AND MARITIME CRIME: HISTORICAL AND MODERN CASE STUDIES

URL Address: http://cdm16064.contentdm.oclc.org/cdm/singleitem/collection/p266901coll4/id/3003/rec/3
Site Summary: Pirates have plied their nefarious trade of robbing, kidnapping, and sometimes killing people at sea since the earliest legitimate traders navigated rivers and oceans in search of commerce. The nineteenth century witnessed the golden age of piracy with the Barbary pirates menacing U.S. trade to such an extent that President Thomas Jefferson declared war on them. Throughout the past three centuries, there have been traditional piracy global hot spots, but none have aroused nations to action until pirates off the coast of Somalia began to routinely attack oil tankers and containerships, holding their crew and cargo for considerable ransoms. This site provides lengthy historical and contemporary case studies that are filled with embedded and tabulated data about the scope and extent of this ages old form of crime.

Critical Thinking Questions and Activities

1. Scroll to page twenty-two and note the data displayed in "Table 2 Piracy Reports, South China Sea Region, 1992-2008." Which countries in the South China Sea region have experienced the most piracy from 1992 to 2008? Juxtapose the years when piracy was abnormally high for these countries with a timeline of historical events. What political and economic conditions may have contributed to the increase in piracy in this region?
2. Scroll to page seventy-seven and note the data displayed on "Table 1 Piracy Reports between November 1958 and October 1959." Why were piracy rates so high in this area during this time period? Research the territorial dispute between Indonesia and Malaysia during this time. How might this conflict have contributed to the high piracy rate?
3. Scroll to page 104 and read the chapter "The Looting and Rape of Vietnamese Boat People." Select embedded data and employ it to show the positive correlation between the end of the Vietnam War and the increase in piracy.
4. Scroll to page 196 and read the chapter titled "Guns, Oil and Cake: Maritime Security in Guinea." Examine "figure 1" on page 197 titled "Gulf of Guinea Piracy and Armed Robbery against Ships, 2003 - 2007." Explain why Nigeria is experiencing the highest rates of piracy during this time. Assume that you are the president of Nigeria. How would you reduce the number of piracies? Explain what the consequences may be if you fail.

Related Internet Sites

Economics of Piracy: Pirate Ransoms and Livelihoods Off the Coast of Somalia
   http://www.geopolicity.com/upload/content/
pub_1303037666_regular.pdf
   This document contains embedded data that shows the business aspect of piracy among Somali pirates.
The International Maritime Bureau
   http://www.icc-ccs.org/piracy-reporting-centre
   Provides statistics on the latest acts of piracy throughout the world along with relevant maps and other data.

STATISTICAL MATERIALS FOR LEARNING ABOUT JAPAN

URL Address: http://www.stat.go.jp/english/data/chouki/index.htm

Site Summary: Finding historical and social sciences quantitative data about Asian countries can be a challenge because the sites often lack an English translation. This English-language gateway site about Japan is divided into four statistical sections: (1) "The Japan Statistical Yearbook" contains recent, census-like data about the land, population, economy, culture, society, and monetary policy; (2) "Japan Monthly Statistics" features similar statistical information for several years, but the data is also displayed on a monthly basis; (3) "The Statistical Handbook of Japan" furnishes tables, figures, maps, and photographs to present more of an overview of all of the collected data; and (4) "Historical Statistics of Japan" contains data about the same key components of the previous sections, but it dates back to 1868.

Critical Thinking Questions and Activities

1. Click on "Historical Statistics of Japan." Select "Chapter 31 Defense." Click on "31-1 National Defense Expenditure (F.Y. 1950-2006)." Scan the total amounts in yen that Japan has spent for national defense. Explain why it was so small during the 1950s and 1960s. Why has it steadily increased since the 1970s? Discuss the advantages and disadvantages of Japan's small national defense expenditures in terms of Japan's economic progress and its vulnerability to aggression from surrounding Asian countries.

2. Click on "Historical Statistics of Japan." Select "Chapter 25 Education." Click on "25-14 Educational Expenditure by Founder and Source of Funds (F.Y. 1949-2004)." Compare the amount spent on schools for a group of chosen years and compare the amounts to that spent for national defense for the same span of years. What do the expenditure amounts tell you about Japan's priorities?

3. Click on "Statistical Handbook of Japan," and select "Population." Scroll to "2. Declining Birth Rate and Aging Population." Employ the population pyramid data to launch a class discussion about the social, economic, employment, and medical problems that Japan faces due to a declining birthrate and an aging population. After exploring the problems that Japan must deal with in the future, initiate a discussion regarding possible solutions. Prior to beginning the solutions phase of the class discussion, ask the students to research Japan's progress with robotics and their position about allowing "guest workers" or immigrants to their country.

4. Select "Japan Statistical Yearbook," and click on "Chapter 21 Health and Sanitation." Select "21-1 Intake of Nutrition." Compare the number of daily calories that the average Japanese consumed in 2008 with that of Americans. Write a blog entry and use the statistics to pose some questions about the potential longevity of Japanese versus

Americans. Explore what responsibility governments should have for the health of their citizens.

Related Internet Sites

NationMaster.com
http://www.nationmaster.com/country/ja-japan
Furnishes useful, current comparative statistics not only for Japan but for every country in the world. This site is helpful for responding to questions 2 and 4.

Statistics Bureau of Japan
http://www.stat.go.jp/english/
This site contains daily statistical data about the Japanese economy.

STATISTICS CANADA

URL Address: http://www.statcan.gc.ca/start-debut-eng.html
Site Summary: Canada is such a diverse country in its people and culture that it thinks of itself more as a federation rather than a nation. Sparsely populated in comparison to its size, with a climate ranging from temperate to Arctic, it is a land of vast natural resources in gold, oil, uranium, and timber. Unlike other countries, it conducts a census every five years rather than ten. It also surveys the population with additional questions about all areas of Canadian life. This site provides the findings from the latest census that are searchable by keyword, broad subject areas, and key resources. The latter format includes data tables, maps, articles, and reports.

Critical Thinking Questions and Activities

1. Under "Statistics by Subject," select "Health" and click on the link "Life Expectancy and Deaths." Click on "Summary Tables." View the table titled "Life expectancy at birth and at age 65, by sex and by province and territory." What is the average life span of both sexes at birth? Compare this age to life expectancy at birth for U.S. citizens. Canada has government-sponsored national healthcare for its citizens. Research the impact that this system may have on the longevity of Canadians. Click on the subtopic "health care services" for additional help answering these questions.
2. Under "Statistics by Subject," select "Aboriginal peoples." Click on "population statistics" and select "Education literacy and skills." Employ some of the tabulated data concerning Aboriginal educational rates and compare them to that of the non-Aboriginal population.

Write a research paper about the educational challenges that Canada faces with regard to its aboriginal population.
3. Under "Statistics by Subject," select "Languages," and click on the link "French language groups." What areas of Canada declare French versus English as their mother tongue? Research the role that language played in Quebec's desire to secede from the rest of Canada. Explain how the people of Quebec fear the loss of their language and culture.
4. Under "Statistics by Subject," select "Crime and Justice." Click on the link "Crime and Justice (general)." Choose "Latest news releases in the Daily," and click on the link "Aboriginal people as victims and offenders June 6, 2006." Read the entire report about crime and justice involving Aboriginal people in Canada. What types of criminal and judicial problems do they suffer from in greater proportion than non-Aboriginal people? Imagine that you are a social scientist who has been tasked with making recommendations to reduce the number of crimes and judicial incidents involving aboriginal people. What recommendations would you make to the Canadian government?

Related Internet Sites

Government of Canada
http://www.gc.ca/home.html
The official government site of Canada features some helpful overview links under the heading "About Government."
Key Development Forecasts for Canada
http://www.ifs.du.edu/ifs/frm_CountryProfile.aspx?Country=CA
Provides useful extrapolated data about Canada's population, energy needs, environmental challenges, and health concerns.

THE SURVEY OF SCOTTISH WITCHCRAFT 1563 TO 1736

URL Address: http://www.shc.ed.ac.uk/Research/witches/index.html
Site Summary: The Scottish witch-hunts lasted for several centuries. During this period, more than one thousand people were executed as witches. More than four thousand were accused. The majority of witches were women. Most were older, widowed, and poor. Although the exact cause of these witch-hunts will remain a mystery, some of them coincided with stressful economic times and during periods when the church was trying to assert itself over the state. This outstanding database contains four thousand records of accused witches. It is searchable by name, date, place, or accusatory categories. Developed by the Scottish Economic and Social Research Council and the University of Edinburgh, the site also provides the means to convert collected data into interactive graphs and maps for display purposes.

Critical Thinking Questions and Activities

1. Click on the "Database" tab and choose "Search the database." Elect "Search for accused witches by name, place." In the search box, choose "male." For "Socioeconomic status," elect "Lairds/Barons." Click on "Search Accused." The lairds and nobility accounted for only 6 percent of those accused of witchcraft. Read the case histories of the three accused men resulting from your search. Clear the search form and search the following variables: "female," "very poor," and "parish." Compare the circumstances that caused the lairds/baron to be accused versus the very poor females. What patterns can you detect?

2. Click on the "Database" tab and then the link "Search for cases of witchcraft by date and characterization." In the characterization box, choose "midwifery." Read the resulting ten cases histories. What other common denominators can you find besides midwifery as a possible cause of accusation? Return to the "Accused witches" search box. Type the name of each accused into the search box and note other variables such as socioeconomic status, age, gender, and place of residence. Explain why some historians have proposed that midwives and folk healers may have been at greater risk for accusation.

3. Click on the "Database" tab and then the link "Search for witchcraft trials by date and place." There were four panic periods when significant numbers of people were accused of being witches: 1590 to 1591, 1628 to 1630, 1649, and 1661 to 1662. Choose two of the dated episodes and read the resulting case histories. Can you find any commonalities among the accused?

4. Click on the "Database" tab and then the link "Search for Accused Witches." Under "marital status," choose "widowed." This status accounted for 19 percent of those accused. Search the resulting case histories of widows who were accused of being witches. Some historians surmise that widows may have been in competition for employment with men during hard economic times. What occupations are listed for each accused? Are these jobs that could also have been worked by men? Are there any other factors that widows seem to share that may account for their high accusal rate?

Related Internet Sites

The Dammed Art Witchcraft and Demonology
    http://www.gla.ac.uk/services/specialcollections/virtualexhibitions/
damnedart/

Contains images of primary source books that document the extent of the witchcraft problem in Scotland, Switzerland, Germany, and the Low Countries in the seventeenth century.

The Horrid Sinne of Witchcraft: The Scottish Witch-Hunt in Burgh Records
http://www.scan.org.uk/exhibitions/witchhunt_contents.htm
Provides images of documents that illustrate the role of witchcraft in seventeenth century Scotland.

TRANS-ATLANTIC SLAVE TRADE DATABASE

URL Address: http://www.slavevoyages.org/tast/index.faces
Site Summary: The Atlantic slave trade began in the 1500s and lasted until 1860. Essentially, it involved Europeans and North Americans trading goods and guns for African slaves. Once purchased in Africa, the slaves were shipped across the Atlantic to the West Indies, Central America, and South America. During this period, approximately ten to fifteen million enslaved people underwent a journey known as the Middle Passage. This web site provides listings and tables of specific voyages plus interactive software that permits users to analyze the full extent of the trade in numbers of slaves transported and sold.

Critical Thinking Questions and Activities

1. Select "Search the Voyages Database." Click on the "Tables" tab. In the "Rows" search box, select "100-year periods" from the drop-down menu. In the "columns" search box, select "Region where voyage began." In the "cells" search box, choose "Sum of disembarked slaves." Click on "Show." Which countries were dominant in the transatlantic slave trade during each of the respective centuries? Research the main reasons why the dominant countries changed over the centuries. Be sure to include information about the passage of abolition laws by some nations.
2. Click on "Search the Voyages Database." Click on the "Customs graphs" tab. In the "X axis" search box, select "African Resistance" from the drop-down menu. In the "y axis," select "Number of Voyages." Click on "Pie graphs." Explain why the number of African resistance acts during these centuries was so insignificant. Research how slaves were transported and maintained on the ships.
3. Click on "Search the Voyages Database." Select the "Tables" tab. In the "Rows" search box, choose "5 year periods." In the "columns" search box, select "Broad region where voyage began." In the "cells"

search box, choose "sums of embarked slaves." What years were the peak years for the slave trade for European countries? Laws were passed abolishing international trafficking in slaves as early as 1807. The United States banned slave trading in 1820 (see *Ending the Atlantic African Slave Trade* http://histclo.com/act/work/slave/ast/astatle.html). Why is there a dramatic drop in the slave trade for European countries only after 1830? Why is there an increase in slave trading in Brazil after these laws were enacted?

4. Click on "Search the Voyages Database." Select the "Timeline" tab. For the "display" variable, choose "Average slave deaths." Click on "Show." Move the cursor to the right to see the total number of slave deaths per year. Which spans of years were the most life-threatening for slaves trying to survive the Middle Passage? Investigate why these years were more dangerous than others.

Related Internet Sites

Mortality and the Transatlantic Slave Trade
http://www.collegeboard.com/prod_downloads/yes/4297_MOD-ULE_12.pdf
Provides a data-driven lesson plan that uses the Voyages database to determine the variables that may or may not have affected slave mortality rates.

Trans-Atlantic Slave Trade Voyage Database FAQ
http://www.slavevoyages.org/tast/help/faq.faces
Provides easy-to-understand questions and answers concerning how to use the graphs, tables, and the query part of the database.

TRENCHES ON THE WEB (1914 TO 1918) CASUALTY FIGURES

URL Address: http://www.worldwar1.com/tlcrates.htm
Site Summary: *Trenches on the Web* is a well-maintained and well-organized multimedia site for historical information about World War I. This war had some of the deadliest combats in human history, claiming the lives of more than thirty-seven million people. New kinds of weapons including heavy artillery, machine guns, tanks, flamethrowers, and even the use of poison chlorine gas ensured millions of casualties. Much of the war was fought by soldiers encased in trenches that were seven feet deep by six feet wide and topped by barbed wire. Ordered by their commanding generals to attack the enemy by surmounting the trenches, exposed troops faced withering machine gun assaults from the opposing side. This site provides lists of casualties for each warring country and accompanying graphs.

Critical Thinking Questions and Activities

1. Under "Sorted by Number Mobilized," click on the table graph. Research why Russia lost almost as many troops as Germany. Write a paper about how these losses may have been one of the causes of the Russian Revolution.
2. Great Britain initially declared its neutrality at the outset of the war until Germany invaded Belgium. A mutual defense pact between the two countries forced Great Britain into the war. Scroll to the table titled "Sorted by number dead" and click on the "graph" link. Employ the data about Great Britain's losses to argue that Great Britain should not have honored their defense pacts and remained neutral during the war.
3. Under "Sorted by number dead" and "Sorted by Percent wounded of total mobilized," study the losses for France. Research how long it took France to surrender to Germany at the outbreak of World War II. How may the number of casualties France suffered during World War I have influenced their decision?
4. Under "Sorted by number dead," total the number of dead from Germany, Austria-Hungary, Turkey, and Bulgaria. Research why these countries lost fewer troops than Allied countries, but eventually lost the war.

Related Internet Sites

France at War
http://www.worldwar1.com/france/france2.htm
Contains some links to data about profits and swindles during World War I as well as information about trench warfare, battles, and French losses. This site is useful for answering question 3.
Trenches on the Web Library
http://www.worldwar1.com/reflib.htm
Provide an excellent overview of the events surrounding World War I and related links to specific aspects of the war, including casualty rates.

U.S. AND ALLIED EFFORTS TO RECOVER AND RESTORE GOLD AND OTHER ASSETS STOLEN OR HIDDEN BY GERMANY DURING WORLD WAR II

URL Address: http://fcit.usf.edu/holocaust/resource/gold/gold.pdf
Site Summary: This 259-page preliminary report, commissioned by President William Clinton in 1997, details the theft by Nazi Germany of an estimated $580 million of gold (or about $5.6 billion in today's currency) in

addition to other indeterminate amounts during World War II. The funds were stolen from governments and civilians in the countries that Germany conquered, particularly from Jewish victims who were murdered in extermination camps and whose gold fillings in their teeth were used to increase Nazi Germany's war coffers. Although there are some tabulated data in this site, much of the shocking revelatory finances are embedded within the findings and summarized from searching more than five million pages of recently de-classified reports and documents.

Critical Thinking Questions and Activities

1. Scroll to page xli of the report. Note the tables titled "Estimates in the Allied Swiss Negotiation" and "External German Assets (Excluding Gold)." What amount has Switzerland paid so far to victims of the Holocaust, reparations, and to the Tripartite Gold Pool? Imagine that you are a negotiator for the Tripartite Gold Pool. Employ the data displayed in these two tables to argue that Switzerland should pay more.

2. Switzerland was a neutral country during World War II. The report states, however, that "neutrality collided with morality." Employ the figures displayed in the table titled "Swiss Estimates of German Assets in Switzerland" on page xliii to explain the truth in the quoted statement. How did Switzerland's financial dealings with the German Reich actually help prolong the war?

3. Scroll through pages 147 to 149 of the report titled "Swiss Contribution to Non-Repatriable Victims of the Nazi." Extract the embedded financial figures in the report and use them to explain the financial shenanigans that Switzerland engaged in to forestall payment. Explain the effect it had upon Jewish organizations that were attempting to help Jewish non-repatriable victims to emigrate to Palestine.

4. Scroll through pages 175 to 179 that discuss Allied negotiations with Portugal. Extract the relevant financial figures to show how neutral Portugal's complicity with the Third Reich's war machine, by accepting gold payments in exchange for tons of wolfram, mica, tin, chrome, and antimony, assisted the Third Reich in manufacturing advanced weapons. Explain why the United States compromised on the final payment with Portugal in exchange for access to an airbase in the Portuguese Azores.

Related Internet Sites

Searching for Records Relating to Nazi Gold Part II

http://www.archives.gov/research/holocaust/records-and-research/
searching-records-relating-to-nazi-gold2.html
Although this site does not contain quantitative data, it gives an excellent
overview of the gripping story about how the Allies went about unraveling
the accounts that showed where the trail of Nazi gold led.
Report of the Swiss Bergier Commission
http://www.uek.ch/en/
As a result of the 1997 report, Switzerland agreed to establish a commission to inquire further about its finances and dealings with Nazis during
World War II. The report does contain embedded financial data that updates
the Eizenstat report commissioned by President Clinton.

A VISION OF BRITAIN THROUGH TIME

URL Address: http://www.visionofbritain.org.uk/
Site Summary: Designed by Humphrey Southall and the Great Britain
Historical Geographical Information Location System, this site aggregates
historical survey numbers in the form of historical census data, travel writing, and statistical atlases from 1801 through 2001. Searchable by places,
postal code, or theme, *A Vision of Britain Through Time* contains statistical
information from two centuries concerning British industry, agriculture and
land use, housing, social structure, life and death, ancestry and religion,
population, education, work and poverty, and political life. History and social
sciences students will find a wealth of quantitative data to analyze for historical and social trends research projects.

Critical Thinking Questions and Activities

1. Under "Election results," click on "1983 Thatcher's Landslide." Explain how the Labour Party's platform ensured such a big win for the
   Tory Party in 1983. Use the "Votes" and "Seats" pie charts to analyze
   how the Conservatives garnered most of the seats and votes. Click on
   the link titled "See the Election results mapped by constituency." Use
   the directional and enlargement arrows to zoom in on geographical
   areas of the map. Although Prime Minister Thatcher won in a landslide, there were several areas in Great Britain that voted for the Labour Party. Identify these areas and use the place search feature of the
   database to obtain demographic information that sheds light on why
   they elected to vote for the Labour Party.
2. Click on "Statistical Atlas," followed by the "male unemployment
   link." Lack of work was a twentieth-century problem that plagued
   Great Britain as well as other countries. Some parts of a country can

experience chronic unemployment, which becomes a challenge for governments to remedy. Scroll to the "Options (reloads page)," and record areas of Great Britain that have experienced unemployment beyond 15.91 percent for the 1931, 1951, 1971, 1981, 1991, and 2001 census years. Locate specific places by using the "zoom" and additional navigation features of each corresponding downloaded map. Use other parts of the "Statistical Atlas" and census data to determine what demographic and social variables may have affected male unemployment in these areas.

3. Click on "Statistical Atlas," and choose "Social Structure." Click on "percentage of working age males in Class 1 and 3." Class 2 is considered middle class in the Great Britain census classification. Scroll down to "Options (reloads page)," and obtain similar data for the 1841 to 2001 census years. Create a histogram for the middle class social structure for Great Britain over two centuries, showing how the proportion has increased and or decreased during these time periods. Why does it behoove a country to have a substantial proportion of the population be considered middle class? Discuss the economic and social hazards of inequality among the three main social classes.

4. Click on "Statistical Atlas," and choose "Roots & Religion." Muslims were the largest of the non-Christian religions in the Great Britain 2001 census, but they only represented 2.78 percent of the total population. Use the enlargement and navigation features on the corresponding religion map to determine where Muslims are more than 5 percent of the population. Research how these areas of England have coped with an increase in people denominating themselves as practicing Muslims. Why have some areas in Great Britain adjusted more peacefully to these changes than others? What should or can the government do with these potential hot spot census areas to help all members of the community adjust to changes in the practice of different religions?

Related Internet Sites

British History Online
http://www.british-history.ac.uk/
Provides surveys, documents, maps, and census data concerning British history from medieval to modern times.
The Victorian Census Project
http://www.staffs.ac.uk/schools/humanities_and_soc_sciences/census/
vichome.htm
Contains computerized source documents such as census maps and vital registration statistics related to mid-nineteenth century Great Britain and Ireland. It is an excellent source for comparative historical topics and research.

References

African Activist Archive. (n.d.). Retrieved from: http://africanactivist.msu.edu/

American FactFinder. (n.d.). Retrieved from: http://factfinder2.census.gov/

Association of American Colleges and Universities. (2009). *VALUE: Valid Assessment of Learning in Undergraduate Education.* Retrieved from: http://www.aacu.org/value/metarubrics.cfm

Ayres, I. (2007). *Super-crunchers: Why thinking-by-numbers is the new way to be smart.* New York: Bantam.

Bertin, J. (2011). *Semiology of graphics, diagrams, networks and maps.* Redlands, CA: ESRI Press.

Bolker, E., & Mast, M. (2013). *Common sense mathematics.* Retrieved from: http://www.cs.umb.edu/~eb/qrbook/qrbook.pdf

Bolton, P. (2009, January). Chart format guide. Retrieved from: http://www.parliament.uk/briefing-papers/SN05073

Bolton, P. (2010, July). Statistical literacy guide how to spot spin and inappropriate use of statistics. Retrieved from: http://www.parliament.uk/briefing-papers/sn04446.pdf

Burdett, A.M., & McLoughlin, T. (2010, July). Using census data in the classroom to increase quantitative literacy and promote critical sociological thinking. *Teaching Sociology* 38 (7), 247–257.

Bureau of Justice Statistics. (2013). Retrieved from: http://www.bjs.gov/

Bureau of Justice Statistics Identity Theft. (n.d.) Retrieved from: http://www.bjs.gov/index.cfm?ty=tp&tid=42

Cantor, N., and Schneider, R.I. (1968). *How to study history.* New York: Thomas Y. Crowell.

Carleton's Quantitative Inquiry, Reasoning, and Knowledge (QUIRK) Initiative. (2009, July). Retrieved from: http://serc.carleton.edu/quirk/index.html

Carlson, L.C. (1981). *Indians, bureaucrats, and land: The dawes act and the decline of indian farming.* Westport, CT: Greenwood Press.

Carnevale, A.P., Smith, N., & Strohl, J. (2010, June). "Projection of Jobs and Educational Requirements through 2018." Retrieved from: http://www9.georgetown.edu/grad/gppi/hpi/cew/pdfs/State-LevelAnalysis-web.pdf

"The Case for Quantitative Literacy." (2001). Retrieved from: http://www.stolaf.edu/people/steen/Papers/01case-for-ql.pdf

Center for Mathematics and Quantitative Electronic Bookshelf at Dartmouth. (n.d.). Retrieved from: http://www.math.dartmouth.edu/~mqed/eBookshelf/

The Chernobyl Catastrophe: Consequences on Human Health. (2006). Retrieved from: http://www.greenpeace.org/international/Global/international/planet-2/report/2006/4/chernobyl-healthreport.pdf)

Children's Defense Fund. (2012). Retrieved from: http://www.childrensdefense.org/
China Data Center. (n.d.). Retrieved from: http:// chinadatacenter.org/
Cohen, B., & Greenfield, J. (1998). *Ben & Jerry's double-dip: How to run a values-led busi-
ness and make money, too.* New York: Simon & Schuster.
Cleveland, W.S. (1985). *The elements of graphing data.* Monterey, CA: Wadsworth Advanced
Books and Software.
Cold War Air Defense Relied Upon Widespread Dispersal of Nuclear Weapons. (2010, No-
vember 16). Retrieved from: www.gwu.edu/~nsarchiv/nukevault/ebb332/
Common Core State Standards Initiative. (2012). Retrieved from: http://www.corestandards.
org/ELA-Literacy/RH/9-10
Craver, K.W. (1994). *School library media centers in the 21st century changes and challenges.*
Westport, CT: Greenwood Press.
Darcy, R., & Rohrs, R.C. (1995). *A guide to quantitative history.* Westport, CT: Praeger.
De Lange, J. (2003). Mathematics for literacy. In: B. Madison and L.A. Steen (eds.), *Quantita-
tive literacy: Why numeracy matters for schools and colleges (pp. 75–89).* Princeton, NJ:
National Council on Education and the Disciplines.
DIG Stats. (n.d.). Retrieved from: http://www.cvgs.k12.va.us:81/DIGSTATS/
Earthtrends. (n.d.) Retrieved from: http://www.wri.org/project/earthtrends/
EuroStat. European Commission. (2013, August 11). Retrieved from: http://ec.europa.eu/euros-
tat
Evans, R.J. (1999). *In defense of history.* New York: W.W. Norton & Company.
Feinstein, C.H., & Thomas, M. (2002). *Making history count a primer in quantitative methods
for historians.* New York: Cambridge University Press.
Floud, R. (1977, April). Quantitative history: Evolution of methods and techniques. *Journal of
the Society of Archivists* 5, 407–417.
Fogel, R.W. (1975, April). The limits of quantitative methods in history. *American Historical
Review* 80, 329–349.
Freeland, C. (2012). *Plutocrats: The rise of the new global super-rich and the fall of everyone
else.* New York: Penguin Press.
Gal, I. (1997). Numeracy: Imperatives of a forgotten goal. In: L.A. Steen (ed.) *Why numbers
count* (pp. 36–44). New York: College Entrance Examination Board.
GapMinder. (2005, February 25). Retrieved from: http://www.gapminder.org/
Global Statistics World Community Grid. (2013, November 8). Retrieved from: http://
www.worldcommunitygrid.org/stat/viewGlobal.do
Goodare, J., et al. (2003). Survey of Scottish witchcraft. Retrieved from: http://www.shc.ed/
ac.uk/Research/witches/reading.html
Grawe, N.D. (2011, Spring). Beyond math skills: Measuring quantitative reading in context.
New Directions for Institutional Research 149, 41–52.
Grawe, N.D. (2012, Spring). Achieving a quantitatively literate citizenry: Resources and com-
munity to support national change. *Liberal Education* 98, 3–35.
Grawe, N.D., & Rutz, C.A. (2009). The integration with writing programs: A strategy for
quantitative reasoning program development, *Numeracy* 2(2), 1-18.
Grawe, N.D., et al. (2010). A rubric for assessing quantitative reasoning in written arguments.
Numeracy 3(1), 1–21.
Harris Vault. (2013). Retrieved from: http://www.harrisinteractive.com/Insights/Harris-
Vault.aspx
Haskins, L., & Jeffrey, K. (1990). *Understanding quantitative history.* Cambridge, MA: MIT
Press.
Herlihy, D. (1972). Quantification and the middle ages. In V.R. Lorwin & J.M. Price (eds.),
The dimensions of the past (pp. 13–51). New Haven, CT: Yale University Press.
Hersh, R.H. (n.d.). Life isn't a multiple choice question. Retrieved from: http://
www.docstoc.com/docs/91932367/Life-Aint-Multiple-Choice-Questions
High Growth Industry Profile Information Technology. (2010, March 8). Retrieved from: http:/
/www.doleta.gov/brg/indprof/IT_profile.cfm
Historical Census Browser. (2007). University of Virginia. Retrieved from: http://mapserv-
er.lib.virginia.edu/

Historical Tables, Budget of the United States Government, Fiscal Year 2008. (2008). Retrieved from: http://www.gpo.gov/fdsys/search/pagedetails.action?granuleId=&packageId=BUDGET-2008-TAB&fromBrowse=true

Historical Tables, Budget of the United States Government, Fiscal Year 2008, National Debt. (2008). Retrieved from: http://www.gpo.gov/fdsys/search/pagedetails.action?granuleId=&packageId=BUDGET-2008-TAB&fromBrowse=true

History Matters. (2013). George Mason University. Retrieved from: http://historymatters.gmu.edu/mse/numbers/question4.html

Hudson, P. (2000). *History by numbers an introduction to quantitative approaches.* New York: Oxford University Press.

Jordan, J., & Haines, B. (2003, summer). Fostering quantitative literacy clarifying goals: Assessing student progress. *Peer Review 5*, 16–19.

Kalyvas, S., & Sambanis, N. Bosnia's civil war origins and violence dynamics. In P. Collier and N. Sambanis (eds.) *Understanding civil war evidence and analysis* (pp. 191–222). Washington, DC: The World Bank. Retrieved from: stathis.research.yale.edu/documents/Bosnia.pdf

Klass, G.M. (2012). *Just plain data analysis finding, presenting, and interpreting scientific data.* (2nd edition). New York: Rowman & Littlefield Publishers, Inc.

Kobrin, D. (1996). *Beyond the textbook: Teaching history using documents and primary sources.* Portsmouth, NH: Heineman.

Lorwin, V.R., & Price, J.M. *The dimensions of the past materials, problems, and opportunities for quantitative work in history.* New Haven, CT: Yale University Press.

Mathematical Association of America. (2001). *The case for quantitative literacy.* Retrieved from: http://www.maa.org/ql/001-22.pdf

Mayer-Schonberger, V., & Cukier, K. (2013). *Big data: A revolution that will transform how we live, work, and think.* New York: Houghton Mifflin.

Mehta, T. (2013). Excel tutorials and tips. Retrieved from: http://www.tushar-mehta.com/excel/tips/

The Nanking Massacre Project. (2008). Retrieved from: www.library.yale.edu/div/Nanking/

National Center for Education Statistics. (2005). Create a graph. Retrieved from: http://nces.ed.gov/nceskids/createagraph/

National Numeracy Network. (2013). Retrieved from: http://serc.carleton.edu/nnn/index.html

NationMaster: Where Statistics Come Alive. (2013). Retrieved from: http://www.nationmaster.com/

NCAA Sports Statistics. (2013). Retrieved from: http://www.ncaa.org/wps/wcm/connect/public/NCAA/.../Stats/index.html

O'Day, K. (2008). Data visualization and Excel charts. Retrieved from: http://processtrends.com/TOC_data_visualization.htm

Paul, R. (1993). *Critical thinking: What every person needs to survive in a rapidly changing world.* Santa Rosa, CA: Foundation for Critical Thinking.

Peltier, J. (2013). Charting in Microsoft Excel. Retrieved from: http://peltiertech.com/Excel/Charts/

The Peter G. Peterson Foundation. (2013). Retrieved from: www.pgpf.org/

Pope, A. (2012). Charting examples. Retrieved from: http://www.andypope.info/charts.htm

Porter, T.M. (1997). The triumph of numbers: Civic implications of quantitative literacy. In L.A. Steen (ed.), *Why numbers count* (pp. 1–10). NY: College Entrance Examination Board.

Reading and Organizing Quantitative Evidence. (2013). Retrieved from: historymatters.gmu.edu/mse/numbers/reading.html

Reich, R. (1991). *The work of nations.* New York: Alfred A. Knopf.

Rycaut, P. (1682). *The history of the present state of the ottoman empire.* Retrieved from: http://books.google.com/books/about/The_History_of_the_Present_State_of_the.html?id=KKMuTmW98DEC

Scatterplots. (n.d.). Retrieved from: http://mste.illinois.edu/courses/ci330ms/youtsey/scatterinfo.html

Schield, M. (2010). Quantitative graduation rates at U.S. four-year colleges. Retrieved from: http://wwww.citeseerx.ist.psu.edu/viewdoc/download?doi=10.1.1.158

Skiorskii, A., et al. (2011). Quantitative literacy at michigan state university, 1: development and initial evaluation of the assessment. Numeracy 4 (2), 1–21.

South African Data Archive. (n.d.). Retrieved from: http://sada.nrf.ac.za/

The Spreadsheet Page. (2013). Retrieved from: http://spreadsheetpage.com/index.php/tips

Statistical Materials for Learning about Japan. (2012) Retrieved from: http://rnavi.ndl.go.jp/research_guide/statistical-materials-for-learning-about-japan/

Statistics Online Computational Resource Center University of California, Los Angeles. (2002). Retrieved from: http://www.socr.ucla.edu/

Statistics Canada. (2014). Retrieved from http://www.statcan.gc.ca/start-debut-eng.html

StatLit.org. (2013). Retrieved from: http://www.statlit.org/

Steen, L.A. (ed.). (1977). *Why numbers count: quantitative literacy for tomorrow's America.* New York: The College Board.

Steen, L.A. (1990, Spring). Numeracy. *Daedalus* 119, 211–231.

Steen, L.A. (1999). Numeracy: The new literacy for a data-drenched society. *Educational Leadership* 57, 8–13.

Steen, L.A. (2000, Spring). Reading writing, and numeracy. *Liberal Education* 86, 26–37.

Steen, L.A. (ed.). (2001). *Mathematics and democracy: The case for quantitative literacy.* Washington, DC: Woodrow Wilson Fellowship Foundation. Retrieved from: http://www.maa.org/ql/mathanddemocracy.html

Steen, L.A. (2004). *Achieving quantitative literacy: An urgent challenge for higher education.* Washington, DC: Mathematical Association of America.

Taylor, C.H. (2009). Assessing quantitative reasoning. *Numeracy* 2 (2), 1– 5.

Tobias, S. (1978). *Overcoming math anxiety.* Boston: Houghton Mifflin.

Tobias, S. (1987). *Succeed with math: Every student's guide to conquering math anxiety.* New York: The College Board.

Triangle Shirtwaist Factory Fire. (2013). New York State Investigating Commission. Retrieved from: http://ocp.hul.harvard.edu/ww/nysfic.html

Trilling, B., & Fadel, C. (2012). *21st century skills: Learning for life in our times.* San Francisco: Jossey-Bass.

Trueman, R.E. (1977). *An introduction to quantitative methods for decision making.* (2nd ed.). New York: Holt, Rinehart and Winston.

Tufte, E.R. (1990). *Envisioning information.* Cheshire, CT: Graphics Press.

Tufte, E.R. (1997). *Visual explanations: Images and quantities, evidence and narratives.* Cheshire, CT: Graphics Press.

Tufte, E.R. (2001). *Visual display of quantitative information.* (2nd ed.). Cheshire, CT: Graphics Press.

Tufte, E.R. (2006). *Beautiful evidence.* Cheshire, CT: Graphics Press.

UN Economic Commission for Europe. (2009a). Making Data Meaningful: Part 1. A guide to writing stories about numbers. Retrieved from: http://www.unece.org/fileadmin/DAM/stats/documents/writing/MDM_Part1_English.pdf

UN Economic Commission for Europe. (2009b). Making Data Meaningful Part 2. A Guide to Presenting Statistics. Retrieved from: http:// www.unece.org/stats/documents/writing/MDM_Part2_English.pdf

UN Statistics. (2013). Retrieved from: http://unstats.un.org/

U.S. 21st Century Workforce Commission. (2000, June 1). Retrieved from: http://digitalcommons.ilr.cornell.edu/cgi/viewcontent.cgi?article=1003&context=key_workplace

U.S. Census Bureau Voting Population Measures. (n.d.). Retrieved from: http://www.census.gov/hhes/www/socdemo/voting/index.html

U.S. Department of Justice. (n.d.). *Report to Congress on the Activities and Operations of the Public Integrity Section for 2012.* Retrieved from: http://www.justice.gov/criminal/pin/docs/2012-Annual-Report.pdf

United Kingdom Office for National Statistics. (n.d.). Retrieved from: http://www.ons.gov.uk/ons/index.html

Vision of Britain through Time. (2009). Retrieved from: http://www.visionofbritain.org.uk/

Wallsten, P. (2003, March 21). Senate plan could double high-skilled worker visas. *Washington Post* A4–A5.

Ward, R.M., Schneider, M.C., & Kiper, J.D. (2011). Development of an assessment of quantitative literacy for Miami University. *Numeracy* 4 (2), 1–19.

Wolfe, J. (2010). Rhetorical numbers: A case for quantitative writing in the composition classroom. *College Composition and Communication* 61(3), 434–457.

Index

Afghanistan, 70, 76, 79, 82, 112, 127, 128
Africa, 71–72, 75, 77, 82, 86, 113, 137–138, 148–149, 149–150, 169
African activism, 137–138
African American history, 57, 101–102, 104, 125–126, 127
AIDS, 86
Al Qaeda, 116
American soldiers World War II attitudes, 93–94
ancestry, U.S., 52–54
anti-Jewish policy, 159, 177
anti-Semitism, 158–159, 177
Argentina, 56
apartheid, 137
Argonaut Conference, 1945, 138–140. *See also* Yalta Conference, 1945
Asia, 55, 56, 70, 73, 75, 143–144, 162–164, 169
asylum seeking, 68, 83
atomic bombing, Hiroshima and Nagasaki, 131–132

Baader-Meinhof Group, 81
bar charts and histograms, 42
Berlin airlift, 140–141
biological warfare, 94–95
Bisbee deportation, 95–97
black death, 56
Bosnian Civil War, 141–143
Botswana, 71

Brazil, 75
British Petroleum Deepwater Horizon oil spill, 52

California history, 91–92
Canada, statistics, 171–172
capitalism in Russia, 160
Carleton College, 26
census data. *See* United States Census Bureau
Central America, 121
chart display best practices, 38–40
chart types, 40–46
Chernobyl catastrophe, 145–146
Chicago fire, 121–122
children and youth, 56–57, 57–58, 80, 87–88
China, 55, 70, 75, 162–164
Chiquita Brand International, 146–147
cholera epidemic, 165–166
cities data, 59–60
Cohen, Ben, 61
Cold War, 98–99, 105–106
Columbia, 81, 146–147
Common Core Standards, 2
country data, 69–74
create a graph, 48
crime rates, 59, 62, 89, 167, 172
critical thinking skills, 5

D-Day World War II, 164–165

187

About the Author

Kathleen W. Craver, Ph.D., is head librarian at National Cathedral School in Washington, DC. She is the author of a number of textbooks and reference books, including *School Library Media Centers in the 21st Century* (1994), *Teaching Electronic Literacy* (1997), *Using Internet Primary Sources to Teach Critical Thinking Skills in History* (1999), *Creating Cyber Libraries: An Instructional Guide for School Library Media Specialists* (2002), and *Term Paper Resource Guide to Nineteenth-Century U.S. History* (2008).